T0365921

MEMOIR:
MOVING IN POETRY, PROSE, AND PHOTOS

MEMOIR:
MOVING IN POETRY, PROSE, AND PHOTOS

RACHEL LOUISE CLAY, Ph.D

This book is a work of non-fiction. Unless otherwise noted, the author and the publisher make no explicit guarantees as to the accuracy of the information contained in this book and in some cases, names of people and places have been altered to protect their privacy.

Archway Publishing books may be ordered through booksellers or by contacting:

Archway Publishing
1663 Liberty Drive
Bloomington, IN 47403
www.archwaypublishing.com
844-669-3957

Drrachelclay@comcast.net
540-684-2729 mobile
540-642-4234 home

Because of the dynamic nature of the Internet, any web addresses or links contained in this book may have changed since publication and may no longer be valid. The views expressed in this work are solely those of the author and do not necessarily reflect the views of the publisher, and the publisher hereby disclaims any responsibility for them.

Any people depicted in stock imagery provided by Getty Images are models, and such images are being used for illustrative purposes only. Certain stock imagery © Getty Images.

ISBN: 978-1-6657-7064-4 (sc)
ISBN: 978-1-6657-7065-1 (hc)
ISBN: 978-1-6657-7066-8 (e)

Library of Congress Control Number: 2024926604

Print information available on the last page.

Archway Publishing rev. date: 02/10/2025

To my granddaughter and namesake,
Rachelle D. Adams:

You are a song in tune,
And a flower in bloom.
Our relationship formed late,
But a growing love was worth the wait.

CONTENTS

JONES SIDE

COOPER SIDE

BOTH SIDES

ACKNOWLEDGMENTS

Although my mother passed away in 2003, I thank her for my beginning and for her encouragement as we moved from place to place. Otherwise, I might not have survived the many moves of my childhood. As a child, I could not have had a better encourager. Additionally, I am grateful to her for helping me with my daughter.

I also thank Mildred and Albert "Diz" Russell, the manager and owner, respectively, of the Legendary Orioles vocal group. Together, they carried on the legacy of the original Orioles vocal group that began in Baltimore, Maryland, in 1948 and arguably started rhythm and blues music. We became friends in the early 1990's. I attended many free live entertainment shows, and I met many famous entertainers. Diz passed away in 2016.

Last but not least, thanks to Regina Mays, Karen DeShazo, Corrine Hardison, and Joe and Nancy Peters for their invaluable assistance. Sister Mays taught me how to insert and crop the photographs in my memoir. Karen helped me with other computer applications such as downloading documents. Corrine edited my many manuscript revisions and offered constructive suggestions and feedback. Joe and Nancy encouraged and motivated me from the outset.

I owe a debt of gratitude to everyone who helped me with my memoir. Although I cannot name everyone, a few additional names are Mary Watts, Arnette Thompson, Javon Greene, Gwyn Jackson, Barbara and Paul Cooper, Terry and Ronnie DeVaughn, David Jones, Jr., Pauline Linthicum, Beatrice and Kenneth Martin, Hazel Smith, Deloris James, Michele Cooper, Helen Armstrong, and Madge Haynes.

INTRODUCTION

Gazing out of the window of my final address, I began to count the number of times I had moved from place to place in my lifetime. I started moving at 19 months old, and by the time I graduated from high school, I had attended 14 schools—15 if I had included kindergarten. My dad was a career soldier; however, the number of schools I attended had little to do with the military. I eventually purchased a house and moved several times during my home ownership. Later on, I sold my house and continued to move. When I had finished counting the moves, the final tally was 37, and I was neither a vagabond, a gypsy, nor a nomad. I decided to write my memoir to revisit and share some of my experiences at my different residences and to explore the effect moving had on me.

> *Why so many addresses?*
> *How had I been effected?*
> *Read on to learn*
> *The twists and turns.*

ONE

MAMA

My mama, Mary Everene "Rene" Cooper, was the middle child of ten, born on May 17, 1925, to Mary Ann Jones and John Reed Cooper, Sr. Since Mama and her mother had the same first name, people called her Rene to distinguish them. Mama's parents were born in

Mama

Evington, Virginia, but eventually migrated to Chattaroy, West Virginia, where Mama grew up. Mary Ann Jones transitioned to Heaven at age 36 on April 1, 1936. She died from a pulmonary embolism following a hysterectomy; she had fibroid tumors. (I was able to obtain

John Reed Cooper, Sr.

a copy of her death certificate from the West Virginia State Department of Health.) Mama turned 11 the following month. Mama said when she heard the news, she thought someone was playing a cruel April Fool's Day joke. No one had a picture or a description of my grandmother.

When their mother went to her Heavenly home,
None of her eight children were grown.
The oldest was sixteen, the youngest two.
What would their father do?

Three different families raised Mama's three younger female siblings after their mother's death. An aunt was already raising her elder sister; two sisters had died young. Her elder and middle brothers stayed home and joined the Army in the early 1940s during World War II. Mama's youngest brother was in a mental health hospital.

Nobody wanted the responsibility of raising Mama. She told me she had contracted rheumatic fever at age seven, leaving her with an enlarged heart, and her doctor barred her from strenuous activity. A woman Mama called "the granny lady" nurtured her, while her father worked in the coal mine. With the granny lady's help, Mama said she thrived and did well in school. However, at the end of the tenth grade, she decided not to return to school. Instead, she wanted to leave Chattaroy to live in Baltimore, Maryland where she had relatives. Her father gave consent, and Mama left home in the summer of 1941. Rumor had it that the 16-year-old Cooper girl was busty, shapely, and sassy.

Within seven months, Mama was pregnant with me, she said, and because of her heart condition, she wrote to her mother's elder sister, Louise, in Evington, Virginia, and asked to live with her. Aunt Louise traveled to her daughter's house in Washington, D.C., and told Mama to meet her there. Baltimore was about 45 minutes from Washington, D.C., by bus. When Mama arrived in D.C., she said her aunt examined her neck and somehow determined she was, indeed, pregnant; she took Mama to live with her.

TWO

HAD YOU HEARD

On Sunday, October 18, 1942, on the heels of General Douglas MacArthur's escape from the Philippines, the beginning of the Battle of Stalingrad, and the Battle of

 Midway, I entered the world— smack dab in the middle of World War II. Mama said her heart condition gave the local midwife, Lucy Martin, pause.

Louise Martin

Louise Martin

Therefore, Dr. Charles W. Haden delivered me in Evington, Virginia in her aunt Louise Martin's bedroom.

Mama said she named me Rachel in honor of her great- grandmother, who died in slavery. Her grandmother, Bertha "Bert" Jones, told her what her moth-

 er's name was. Bertha Jones was born October 22, 1870, and died August 16, 1942, two months before my birth. She was an only child and had seven children:

Bertha Jones

Richard Hansom, Louise, Gladys, Charles

Henry, Watsi Louis, my grandmother, Mary Ann, and William McKinley. See Appendices A-D for photos of her sons. Mama gave me the middle name Louise, in honor of her aunt Louise, who had come for her when she got pregnant and took care of her. My surname was the same as Mama's, Cooper. Everyone called me Little Louise or Little Lou. Mama loved the Little Lulu comic strip, created by Marjorie Henderson Buell in the 1930s, and on occasion called me her Little Lou-Lou. I did not know my first name was Rachel for many years.

> *During World War Two,*
> *I was born on October 18, 1942.*
> *In Evington, the population grew;*
> *My birth added Little Lou.*

My birthplace, Evington, was a small, unincorporated city located in Campbell County. The well-known city of Lynchburg was about 15 miles away. Aunt Louise's son, Watsie (1929–1995), her daughter

Watsie, Courtesy of Kenneth Martin

Gladys Martin-Lynch (1912–1988), and her two sons, Tommy (1928–2018), and Lawrence (1930–2023), were present the day I was born. The boys were ages 12 to 14. A story about the boys that my family told me over the years was that

Gladys

Auntie put the boys outside when the doctor arrived to

deliver me. However, they found a small hole in the wooden house outside of Auntie's bedroom, and were taking turns peeping through

Tommy

Lawrence, Courtesy of Kenneth Martin

the hole to witness my birth. Auntie heard them, went outside with a broom handle, and threatened to "beat the hell out of them" if she caught them again.

The discussion of my birthplace and childhood below was with the help of Mama, my cousins Tommy and

Lawrence, who were present the day I was born, my cousin Mary Watts, whom I lived with later on, and Mama's first cousin Forest Jones (1924–2018). Mary and

Forest Jones, Courtesy of Helen Armstrong

Mary, Courtesy of Mary Watts

Forest were born in Evington and Mary and Forest were born in Evington and Mary has continued to live there. Additionally, family members provided me with pictures.

Although I was born during World War II, the war had little impact on my family. We lived in an agrarian society; we were self-sufficient. Aunt Louise was of mixed race. Beneath her attractive white face, long brunette hair, and ample breasts were kindness and love for her family and fellow men. An apron protected her loose-fitting ankle-length dresses from the dirt and debris of her workday. The towering woman worked like an Energizer bunny. She awakened and wound herself up at the sound of the rooster crowing, worked all day, and slept at night to recharge. Auntie had placed her husband, Great Uncle George Martin, in a mental institution before my birth. He came home occasionally on visits, but I don't remember ever seeing him. As her husband was away most of the time, Auntie became the matriarch of the family. She managed the small farm with her family, who were present the day I was born. Every family member did their share; it was a matter of survival. (All of Auntie's children were grown and gone except Watsie. Her children were: Ernest, George, Eugene, Edward, Josephine, Gladys, Gertrude, Watsie, and Jerry, who was raised by her sister Gladys who lived five miles away.)

Auntie's wooden, tin-roof farmhouse had an elongated porch and a wooden two-seat porch swing at the far right of the photo behind the bush. At the end of the workday, Auntie placed me on her bosom and rocked me in that swing. The house was about a quarter of a mile from the main road.

The House Where I Was Born, Courtesy of Kenneth Martin

Inside of Auntie's house, kerosene lamps lit the rooms, and our water was well water. The kitchen, at the far end of the house, with its wood-burning cast iron stove, was next to the dining and living rooms. The living room was off limits to family except to welcome visitors usually on Sundays after church. It was Southern tradition.

> *The living room was reserved,*
> *For the visitors Auntie served.*
> *Although known for her hospitality,*
> *A warm welcome was her specialty.*

Next to the living room was Auntie's room, where I was born. In that room, there was a stone hearth in front of a large fireplace that heated the house. The wood popped and crackled, and the sweet smell permeated the house. Adjacent to Auntie's room was another bedroom, and just outside of that room, stairs led to an attic with additional sleeping areas.

Although Evington was an agrarian society, there were four nearby stores: Miles, Rosser, Dowdy, and Mattox. The Miles brothers sold items such as farm equipment, fertilizer, seeds, lime, clothing, and some food. Bently Rosser sold some food and clothing. Roy Doddy mostly sold food, and Cass Mattox was a country store similar to a mom-and-pop store. Mattox also received telegrams from a neighboring city and delivered them. All of the stores sold gasoline.

Auntie purchased needed items, that the family didn't

provide for itself, from one of the stores. However, if a family member needed shoes, a neighboring farmer drove Auntie to Lynchburg, to the Craddock Terry Shoe Company, which originated around 1900 and eventually grew to fifth place in the shoe company world. [1] The major impact World War II had on us was that the government provided families with ration cards and war stamps that were required to purchase items such as shoes, coffee, sugar, and other items made from materials needed for the war. In addition to the four stores, Evington also had a U.S. Post Office that delivered Auntie's mail to the fork in the road about four miles from her house. One of the boys rode on horseback to check for mail in Auntie's mailbox.

Auntie also washed and ironed clothing for a neighboring farm in return for a small amount of cash and flour. The farmer regularly dropped a 40-pound sack of flour off on the main road. Each flour sack was made out of a vibrant cotton print fabric each with a different pattern and design; they were pretty. The women used the empty sacks to hand-stitch clothing, quilts, towels, washcloths, curtains, and more. Mama told me I wore stylish flour-sack dresses.

Gladys Martin

In addition to Great-Aunt Louise, her middle sister Great-Aunt Gladys Jones-Martin

---

[1] The Craddock Terry Hotel, Https//www.craddockterryhotel.com/history (accessed 5/28/2004).

(1892–1976), lived five miles away with her husband, Great-Uncle John Thomas Martin (1895–1949). Both sisters had the last name Martin, but the family knew of no relationship. Both sisters were of mixed race, and both were outstanding cooks. However, unlike her towering sister who walked straight up, Great-Aunt Gladys had short legs and hunched over when she walked.

Great-Aunt Gladys and Great-Uncle Johnny had no biological children, but they raised other children. Two of them were Jerry Martin, her sister Louise's youngest son, and another was Mama's elder sister, Eva Cloteal "Clo" Cooper. She turned 21 and left Evington shortly after I was born. She obtained a government job in Washington, D.C.,

Rosie the Riveter

riveting aircraft wings. Mama said Rosie the Riveter had recently become an iconic image symbolizing women who supported the war effort; Aunt Clo was a Rosie.

Other than my two great-aunts and the cousins I lived with, Cousin Irene Martin (1922–2019) walked to

Aunt Louise's almost daily. She lived not far up the road. Aunt Louise's husband was Cousin Irene's uncle. She and Mama were pregnant at the same time.

Irene Martin,
Courtesy of Hazel
Smith

I was born two weeks before her daughter, Phyllis.
Cousin Phyllis was my first playmate.

Cousin Irene visited often.
She and Mama enjoyed talkin'.
As they waited to become mothers,
They comforted one another.

THREE

UPROOTED

Mama told me we were stable in Aunt Louise's house when a well-to-do man proposed to her. They jumped the broom on May 14, 1944. (I found the marriage record on Ancestry.com.). He took us to his farm; I was 19 months old. He had two children from a previous marriage, and his father lived with him. That was my first uprooting. We stayed there until I was almost five years old.

While living on his farm, we visited Aunt Louise most Sundays after church. Visitors gave me money for my piggy bank if I sang the gospel song "Jesus Loves Me." They also gave me money to recite my alphabet and count to one hundred. Years later, Mama confided in me that she didn't want to marry him, but Aunt Louise told her she should

Richard Jones

be grateful that a man of his considerable wealth was interested in her and was willing to help her raise her child. Mama felt obliged to marry him. She said that once married, she had to stay; she had no money and nowhere else to go. She told me her husband was unfaithful and mean to her and that her uncle Richard, her mother's brother, gave her money to leave and told her never to look back.

> *When Mama found a way,*
> *She ended her stay.*
> *She left the thousandaire,*
> *And the nightmare.*

When Mama left her husband, she asked Cousin Eunice, her father's niece, to keep me in Evington until she could go to Washington, D.C., get a job, and get on her feet. She did not take me back to Aunt Louise's because she thought Mama should stay with her husband. With eight children, Cousin Eunice and her husband made room for me. Mary, who helped me with information about my birthplace, was one of them. That was my second uprooting. I did not feel abandoned. I had heard people saying, "Po sickly Rene, she's got that bad heart, and she has to lug that child around. Ain't it a shame? You make your bed hard; you lay in it." I didn't know what that meant, but I did not want to make anything harder for Mama. Mama told me she would come back for me, and I believed her.

Cousin Eunice's daughter, Mary, told me that her mother got me into kindergarten at age four because school started in September and my fifth birthday was not until October. It might have been because I could

recite my alphabet and count to one hundred. Cousin Eunice's son, Walter, who was exactly one month older than me, was eligible to start school. With our brown bag lunches and

Eunice Watts, Courtesy of Mary Watts

Walter Watts, Courtesy of Walter Watts

book bags, we boarded the big yellow school bus together.

Before I completed kindergarten, Mama landed a cook job in a restaurant and came to pick me up from cousin Eunice's. We rode the bus to Baltimore,

Maryland, to the home of her father's sister, Dorothy Cooper (1907–1962), and her husband, James "Shep" Sheppard.

James Sheppard

Uncle Shep Coming Down the White Marble Steps

We climbed beautiful, white marble steps to enter their home. Inside, there was electricity, running water, and an indoor bathroom—something I couldn't have imagined. Living in Baltimore was very different from living in the country. That was my third move.

Heavyset with coarse black hair, Great-Aunt Dorothy's full, no-nonsense face reflected a stern demeanor. Uncle Shep's friendly, fatherly face welcomed me. They had two sons, John 'Papoose' and Jimmy, both older than me, and they kept foster children.

Auntie made it clear that if I misbehaved, she would get butter from the duck (code for spanking). Auntie told Mama she expected her to pick me up every Saturday and spend time with me on weekends. Mama lived and worked in Washington, D.C., 45 miles from Baltimore.

Jimmy, Courtesy of Mary Watts

> *Now that I lived much closer,*
> *Missing Mama was over.*
> *I would be with her*
> *And that was super!*

Mama picked me up from Great-Aunt Dorothy's the following Saturday and every weekend thereafter as long as I lived with Auntie. We rode the bus to Washington, D.C. When we exited the bus, we walked

to a large house with lots of rooms that Mama called a boardinghouse. After she showed me her room, she took me to meet other relatives. We visited Mama's father's brother, Great-

Hester Cooper, Courtesy of Michele Cooper

Jackie Cooper, Courtesy of Michele Cooper

Uncle Jack Winfred Cooper (1903–1951), and his wife, Great-Aunt Hester Winnie-Martin (1902–1998), and their son Jackie (1934–2002), who lived in Washington, D.C. I had not yet met my grandfather, but Mama told me he had three brothers and four sisters: Jack, Willie, Eddie, Amanda, Dorothy, Jane; and Fannie.

We visited Great-Uncle Jack and his family a few times on weekends over the next several months. On

Jackie, Jr., Courtesy of Michele Cooper

one of those visits, we didn't ride the bus; Mama flagged down a yellow taxicab, and I had my first ride in a cab. I noticed that Washington, D.C., did not

Andre, Courtesy of Michele Cooper

have the pretty white marble steps like Baltimore. Jackie eventually had three children: Jackie, Jr., Andre (1961–2008), and Angela Michele. To distinguish between the two, the family called Jackie, Jr., JC. I interacted more with JC in life than with Andre and Michele. JC and I went on vacation to the Hilton Head Resort in South Carolina when we became adults.

Michele Cooper, Courtesy of Michele Cooper

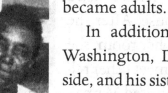

Amanda Thompson, Courtesy of Mary Watts

In addition to meeting family in Washington, D.C., on Mama's father's side, and his sister Dorothy in Baltimore, Mama sometimes took me to meet more of his family in Baltimore before we caught the bus to DC. She took me to meet a second sister, Great-Aunt Amanda, who was also Cousin Eunice's mother with whom I lived in Evington. I also met his niece, Pauline 1917–1990), the daughter of his sister Jane, and Pauline's daughter, Sarah (1935–2018), his great-niece. Sarah and I connected later in life and stayed in contact until her death.

Pauline, Courtesy of Pauline Linthicum, Her Granddaughter

I never met

Sarah, Courtesy of Pauline Lithicum, Her Daughter

Mama's father's other sisters and brothers, nor his father, Jack Cooper, Sr. However, Sarah, pictured above, described him as "a short man with a big round bald head, and the women loved him." See

Me and Sarah

Appendix E for a picture of Mama's father's mother and grandmother.

When we didn't visit relatives and stayed at the boardinghouse, Mama bought food and goodies for us to eat. We also played board games like checkers and card games like Old Maid and War. Sometimes we went to the movies. One movie I recall was The Three Stooges. Occasionally, we shopped for a new dress. On Sundays, Auntie expected me back before dark.

The final weekend with Mama at the boarding-house was Sunday, October 17, 1948, the day before my sixth birthday. Mama returned me to Auntie's earlier than usual on that Sunday. Then, without prior notice, she came on Tuesday to pick me up permanently. She told Auntie she had gotten married on Sunday. Her new husband didn't accompany her; she said he was at work. However, Mama shared the following story with Auntie regarding her new husband:

> I was sitting in the Dunbar Theater in Washington, D.C. watching a movie, and I felt someone touch me on my shoulder. I turned around, and it was Arthur Clay, Lou's father. We had met in 1942 when he passed through Baltimore on his way to World War II and we had lost contact; he had been looking for me since he returned.

Auntie was skeptical. She said, "Arthur Clay wasn't the name I heard regarding Lou's father; you are telling a lie." For the first time, I noticed Mama's double-jointed knees as she took a stance, put her hands on her hips, and boldly retaliated, "I am not lying; nobody knows where I had my pussy but me!"

> *My dad had been anonymous;*
> *Which was the reason for the fuss.*
> *Six years later, he was Arthur Clay.*
> *Auntie said, "No way."*

As for me, I was bursting with joy, as Mama and I gathered my toys and clothing. Like my cousins, I had lived with, I had a father too. On the way to our new address on the bus, Mama apologized for missing my birthday and promised she would not miss another. She also told me I would love my dad and she was looking forward to us being a nuclear family.

FOUR

NUCLEAR FAMILY

My fourth address was the second floor of a house in Washington, D.C., on Seaton Place, NW, where I met my dad for the first time. He, Mama, and I became a nuclear family. We had a front room that Mama set up as a living room, two bedrooms, and a bath. At the front end of the hallway adjacent to the living room were steps leading to the street. The kitchen was at the end of the back end of the hallway, down the steps, and was shared with the landlady.

> I had a mother,
> And I also had a father.
> My dream came true
> To have a nuclear family too.

Our landlady was the first person we knew who had a telephone in 1948. She called someone she knew and demonstrated to me how it worked. She let me say hello and I could hear the person through the earpiece on the phone. My eyes were wide with amazement as I continued to gaze at the telephone. She told my parents that they could use the phone. They didn't know anyone with a phone, but Daddy could call his job if necessary.

My new dad was a World War II veteran and a fit career soldier who shook his shoulders when he chuck-

led. He called Mama by her first name, Mary, instead of Rene, and pronounced it "May-ree." She called him Arthur. Others called Daddy Pop Clay, Sarge, or Buddy.

Sgt. Arthur Clay The way he smoked a Camel cigarette was entertaining. He held it be-

tween his lips until it was mainly ashes. The tiniest bit was left to grab with his fingers as he tried to put it in the ashtray. He missed the ashtray more often than not, and the residue trickled down his

My parents on their wedding day

clothes. How he avoided burning his lips was a mystery.

The first night I slept in my room, I was awakened by what sounded like a hog snorting and rooting for food; it was Daddy snoring. I pulled the cover over my head and put my index fingers in my ears to muffle the sound. The next day, Mama told me I would get used to it. I never did. I didn't understand how she could sleep in the same room with him.

The coming week, Mama took me to Walter Reed Army Medical Center. That was one benefit of her marrying a soldier. She wanted me to have a thorough checkup. I'd never been to a doctor, let alone a hospital. My family had treated me with home remedies such as: rubbing Vicks salve on my chest to relieve congestion from a cold and drinking baking soda water if my stomach was upset. Before Mama left for D.C., she had given me a daily dose of Hadacol to increase my appetite. Hadacol was a liquid tonic that medicine men marketed as a vitamin supplement. I was skinny. She found out that It contained alcohol and stopped giving it to me. It was sweet, and I liked it. I asked her why I couldn't take it anymore. She said, "It made you drunk."

Next, Mama began taking me along when she went to school. After getting married, she left her job as a restaurant cook to enroll in the historic Madam C.J. Walker School of Beauty Culture. She wanted to become a beautician. I played with my toys while she studied. The first day I went with her, we left early, and she took me to meet my aunt Cloteal "Clo" and her husband, Thomas Irvine

Aunt Clo's shapely legs stood out. Uncle Tom's blue-green eyes reminded me of a mixture of Mama's emerald green birthstone ring and the blue sky. Auntie was Mama's elder sister by four years. Uncle Tom and Aunt Clo had identical twin girls named Clarica and

Uncle Tom

Aunt Cloteal

Theresa. Mama told me the stork brought them. That was how she explained to me where babies came from.

 We began to visit Aunt Clo often to help her with the twins. I could not tell them apart until a doctor lanced a boil on Clarica's forehead when she was around

Clarica

Theresa

one year old. It left a tiny mark. However, if their backs were toward me, I still couldn't tell. See Appendix F for an older picture.

> *The only twins in the Cooper Clan*
> *Were Theresa May and Clarica Ann.*
> *They were unique and to adore,*
> *I couldn't have loved them more.*

At Aunt Clo's, I had more playmates than ever before. They taught me games such as hopscotch, hide-and-seek, and Jacks. I also learned how to jump double Dutch rope. One playmate, Bessie May, and I became best friends. She lived in an apartment on the street next to Auntie's. On occasion, instead of playing with our playmates, we played in her apartment. Her mother worked, and we dressed in her clothing and jewelry and put on her makeup. We had fun holding on to the wall and strutting in her high-heeled shoes.

On the days that Mama didn't leave school early to visit Aunt Clo, we caught the bus directly home and passed Seventh and K Streets, NW, where the historical Hahn's Shoe Store stood. In front of Hahn's was a bookstand. If the bus stopped for a red signal light, Mama sent me to buy her an Evening Star newspaper. One evening, as I was handing the seller the nickel for the paper, the bus took off. I tried to catch it. As I approached the next bus stop, Mama was walking toward me. She laughed, "My little Lou-Lou must have flown." I handed Mama her newspaper. We waited for the next bus. After we boarded, Mama read her paper, and I went to sleep.

The first holiday with my nuclear family was Thanksgiving. Daddy had to work, but he picked Mama and me up and drove us to Fort Belvoir for Thanksgiving dinner, and I got to see where he worked. I noticed other soldiers saluted Daddy, and when we got to where he cooked, soldiers called him Pop Clay. We ate in a large dining room with other military families. Daddy couldn't sit down and eat with us, but we were all together in the same place, and the head cook and the man in charge were my dad.

> *Several dishes cooked by Arthur Clay;*
> *Mama called it a buffet*
> *I could choose and go back for more,*
> *I had not eaten that way before.*

For the next holiday which was Christmas, Mama and I decorated a tree together. Daddy was at work, and we didn't wait for him because Mama said he felt decorating a tree was not for him. We finished early and visited Aunt Clo, who had eggnog and cookies for us. We didn't stay long because Mama said Santa would not come until I was asleep. Daddy came home, ate, and we all went to bed early. Among other gifts, Santa brought me an expensive dark blue Chinchilla coat and my first tricycle.

Mama and I also celebrated the next holidays, Easter Sunday and Easter Monday, without Daddy; he had to work. We went to church on Easter Sunday, and the gospel singing made me tap my feet and clap my hands. I had not been to church since I left Cousin Eunice's house in Evington, and I had missed the choir singing. For Easter Monday, Mama filled an Easter basket with dyed eggs, a chocolate bunny, jelly beans, and more, and we went to the Smithsonian National Zoo for Negro Family Day to see the animals and participate in an Easter egg hunt. That historical event started in 1891 because Negroes were prohibited from participating in the White House Easter Egg Roll, which had begun in 1878. [2]

---

[2] Emiley Mallory, "For DC, Easter Monday at the National Zoo is an African-American Tradition," The Root, April 7, 2015, https://www.theroot.com/for-dc-easter-monday-at-the-national-zoo-is-an-african-1790859364 (accessed April 19, 2016).

When Mama saw how much I enjoyed the gospel singing when we went to church on Easter Sunday, she began taking me to gospel concerts. For some reason, Mama had stopped attending church regularly. The first gospel singer I saw in concert was Brother Joe May at Griffith Stadium, where the Washington Senators and the Washington Redskins played ball. The large man sang in a long black robe, and his powerful, high-pitched voice excited the audience. He sang "Search Me, Lord" and became my favorite gospel singer.

The Uline Arena hockey stadium was the next venue on our gospel singing agenda. The singers I remember were Sister Rosetta Tharpe and her partner, Marie Knight. Sister Tharpe played the guitar, and Marie Knight played the piano. The one song I remember them singing was "Up Above My Head, I Hear Music in the Air." I enjoyed the singing. When the concert ended, Mama and I were outside attempting to hail a taxi, and we saw Sister Tharpe. We spoke to her, and she looked at me and said she saw something in me. She asked Mama how she could contact her. She said she wanted to talk to Mama but had another engagement she had to rush off to. Mama gave her our landlady's telephone number. Mama and I were perplexed.

Sister Rosetta Tharpe telephoned Mama and shared that her mother taught her to sing on stage with her as a young child. She asked Mama to entrust me to her so she could teach me to sing with her. Mama asked her if she was a fool and told her she wasn't entrusting a stranger with her little girl. Sister Tharpe hung up, and Mama did not hear from her again. Years later, I learned from reading Sister Tharpe's biography titled "Shout, Sister, Shout!" that in 1949, Sister Tharpe and her singing companion Marie Knight were parting ways, and Sister Tharpe was talent scouting. [3] I surmised that she was thinking of creating a new act where I would sing on stage with her as she had with her mother.

> *The phone call*
> *Was off the wall.*
> *I have wondered, all the same:*
> *If I missed achieving fame?*

An unforgettable incident occurred in early July, shortly after Mama's conversation with Sister Tharpe. Daddy took leave from work to take care of some business in downtown DC, and Mama left me home with him. When he left the house for downtown, I was outside riding my tricycle. Daddy instructed me to go inside. I begged to stay outdoors, and he told me I could play on the porch until he returned. I was not to play on the sidewalk.

Upon Daddy's return, he scolded, "I told you to go

---

[3] Gayle Wald, *Shout Sister Shout: The Untold Story of Rock-and-Roll Trailblazer Sister Rosetta Tharpe* (Boston: Beacon Press, 2007), 99.

in the house; I'm gonna whup you." I followed him inside and reminded him that he said I could play on the porch. He was quiet, and I assumed he remembered the compromise. We ate a sandwich for lunch, and I started back outside. Daddy told me to stay inside. I went to my room and played with my toys.

Daddy fixed dinner, and after I ate, he directed me to go to bed. He waited until I was asleep, snatched the

sheet off me, grabbed me by my underarm with one of his large hands, and began beating me with his other, using a thick leather belt. He grumbled, "Didn't I tell you I was gonna whup you?" When

Young Arthur Clay

he finished hitting me, he had put welts on my body. Some of them bled. As I cried, I thought about how happy I'd been to have a mother and a father, and how proud I was of him for being the head cook where he worked. I had been sheltered, protected, and loved by family members; and they had spanked me lovingly. I recalled Great-Aunt Dorothy's skepticism regarding him being my dad. Doubt also crept into my mind. How could he have been my real Dad?

> *Who would beat their child like that?*
> *He might as well have used a baseball bat.*
> *Mama had spanked me with a belt*
> *Without causing bleeding and welts.*

Mama looked in on me when she came home from school, heard me sniffling, and pulled the cover back. She hurried down the steps to the kitchen, where Daddy was having a snack. I followed her and sat on the steps. She demanded to know why he had beaten me. He replied, "I chastised her because she was hard-headed." Mama grabbed a knife out of the kitchen cabinet drawer. Daddy jumped up from the table and pulled the refrigerator from the wall to create a blockade between them. Mama chased him around it. Unable to catch him, she dragged a chair from the kitchen table and tried to stab him from overhead. She muttered, "You son of a bitch, I will kill you if you ever hit my baby again."

During the fracas, the landlady called the police. A fight between husband and wife, and whipping children was a family affair. However, because the landlady was concerned about damage to her property, two officers responded and talked to my parents. They advised Daddy to leave for the night to allow him and Mama to cool off. He and the policemen left together. I didn't see policemen riding in a squad car or on a motorcycle in the forties; they walked the beat. Although I was comforted that Mama came to my aid the incident frightened me.

When Daddy and the policemen left, I told Mama he could not be my real Daddy. She said he was, and he would not hit me again. Mama cleaned the welts and treated them with salve. My skin eventually healed, but my heart remained welted. From that point on, Mama took me with her everywhere she went. She never left me alone with him again. When we were all at home I played in my room and stayed out of his way.

The next week, Mama had a slight heart attack and an ambulance rushed her to Walter Reed Hospital. She was hospitalized. I was glad that I stayed with Aunt Clo because I was afraid to be at home with Daddy without Mama. Within a week, Mama was discharged and she resumed her normal activities.

The second weekend in August, not long after her discharge from the hospital, she took me to my first annual Evington homecoming. She and I boarded a Trailways motorcoach and headed to Great-Aunt Louise's house. Segregation laws mandated that Mama and I sit in the back of the bus, behind a broad white line across the floor. The bus stopped to allow passengers to stretch and get something to eat. White passengers entered the front door and ate inside. Negro passengers had to go around to the rear, order food and take it back to the bus to eat. I had not known we had to sit at the back of the bus. Other times that we had rode on the bus, I had not noticed because Mama had me by the hand and I sat where she sat. She had to explain the situation to me; when we had to go to the back door of the restaurant to get food. That homecoming bus ride was my first memory of segregation and discrimination at the age of six.

Evington homecoming was when Great-Aunts Louise and Gladys' families gathered in Evington to reconnect, meet new family members, eat, and worship. They were all on Mama's mother's side. Family members took pride in their clothes and how they styled their hair. One could tell they knew they looked good by the way they cocked their heads upward and to the side. Many came in new cars, and most men had money to flash. Great-Aunts Louise and Gladys cooked up a storm. My favorite foods were fried apples with cinnamon, nutmeg, and sugar, thick slabs of fresh fried bacon, chitterlings, pork chops, fried chicken, potato salad, candied yams, rice and bread puddings, and the lip-smacking peach, cherry, and apple cobblers. The idea was to fatten us up, as being skinny was a sign that a family member might not be doing well in the city; they needed to eat heartily during homecoming.

> *Coming from our city homes,*
> *We needed meat on our bones:*
> *We could not get a big belly*
> *From peanut butter and jelly.*

Our annual homecoming wrapped up with families worshipping at Chapel Grove Baptist Church and then breaking bread together in unity and hugging farewell until next year. Mama and I caught the bus home. She had to get me ready to begin first grade. I was almost a year late beginning school as it began in September and I would turn seven in October.

FIVE

SCHOOLS TO MY LOU
NUMBERS 1, 2, AND 3

I compared my primary and secondary school atten-
dance to a square dance tune called, "Skip to My Lou."
My nickname was Lou, and I attended 14 primary and
secondary schools. Therefore, each time I changed
schools, I called it "schools to my Lou." My first, second,
and third elementary "schools to my Lou" were: John
F. Cook in Washington, D.C.; Fort Belvoir in Virginia;
and George Washington Carver back in Washington,
D.C. I completed the last half of first grade at Cook, the
second half at Belvoir, and the second grade through
half of the fifth grade at Carver.

I started Cook Elementary School in September
1949. Mama and I set out together on school days. She
went to her school, and I walked to Cook with two
other students. Mama bought me a red plaid bookbag
and put my brown bag lunch inside. She also showed
me how to catch the bus, and I joined her at her school

at the end of my school day. In the past, Mama and I were always together when boarding a bus, so initially, I was reluctant. Mama encouraged me by telling me I was her big girl and I could do it.

> *Whenever I said, I can't,*
> *Try again, was Mama's chant.*
> *She put the I can gene in place,*
> *Attempting and failing was no disgrace.*

Two months later, Mama finished the course requirements for her cosmetology studies at the Madam C. J. Walker School of Beauty Culture. What was left, was to pass the cosmetology board, which consisted of a written and practical exam. Once she had passed the written exam, she chose me to demonstrate her ability to beautify hair and complete the final part of her requirements. She gave me Shirley Temple curls with bangs and tied a yellow silk ribbon in a bow over my forehead. Mama was the top graduate in her class.

Madam C.J. Walker had an annual parade for the graduates where they rode in red convertible Cadillacs. I was a part of the parade, to show off the hairstyle of the top graduate. I sat with Mama and another graduate where the top was folded down. The Cadillacs moved in a line slowly up 9th  *Me in the Parade* Street, NW for several blocks with horns blowing.

Onlookers lined up on both sides of the street and cheered.

The Saturday after the parade, Mama and Aunt Clo decided to take the twins for a fall stroll. Mama pushed the twins in their double stroller. I rode the tricycle Santa Claus brought me for Christmas. Mama had gotten Daddy to take it to Aunt Clo's. We walked down 49th Street, NE, which was a steep hill. Suddenly, the pedals on my trike started going around too fast for me to keep up, and I lost control. I was headed for Sheriff Road, a heavily trafficked cross street. Miraculously, Mama held onto the twin stroller with one hand and toppled me over with the other. It scared Mama, and she got rid of my trike. I never knew what she did with it. My trike riding was over.

Next, Mama took me downtown to see Santa Claus so that I could tell him what I wanted for Christmas. It  was the second Christmas I lived on Seaton Place and my first time seeing Santa. I wore my Chinchilla Coat Santa brought me last year. I was afraid. He

Me and Santa was a strange-looking man in a red suit with a long white beard. With Mama's prodding, I eventually climbed aboard and recited what I wanted. The first item I asked for was another tricycle. On Christmas Day, Santa bought everything I asked for except the tricycle. Mama said Santa was afraid I would get hurt riding it after what happened with my first trike; I was disappointed.

Following Christmas, during my winter school break, Daddy moved to Fort Belvoir, where he worked and was stationed in the military. He had requested living quarters on the post which had been approved. I didn't want to move. I had just started school in September; I had made friends with classmates, and walking to school with my neighborhood friends was fun. Mama told me that Fort Belvoir was a better place for us to live, and I would like the school there. She encouraged me and made me feel better about moving.

> *Hurdles will always be around;*
> *Disappointments will abound.*
> *But, no matter what might ensue,*
> *You can make it through.*

Fort Belvoir was my fifth residence, and Belvoir Elementary was the second elementary school I attended; I had just begun school three months ago. President Harry S. Truman integrated the military on July 26, 1948, with Executive Order 9981.[4] Negro and white students attended school together on military bases in 1949. I was at the forefront of American inte-

---

[4] Patrick Feng, "Executive Order 9981: Integration of the Armed Forces," National Museum of the United States Army, https://armyhistory.org/executive-order-9981-integration-of-the-armed-forces/, accessed February 10, 2021.

gration law. Segregation laws, of course, remained in effect outside of military walls.

While living at Fort Belvoir, Jewish vendors sold watermelons, vegetables, and fresh fish from horse-drawn wagons. Mama traded with all three and paid each vendor a dollar a week. Each week, the merchants and Mama tallied their books together. One day, the fish wagon man knocked on the door for payment, and Mama had spent his money. She coached me to open the door and tell the man she wasn't home. I opened the door and trumpeted, "My mama said she wasn't home." He smiled and retreated. Mama laughed aloud and said, "That's my little Lou-Lou." I wondered what was funny. I did exactly what she told me.

> *There was no late fee,*
> *And the goods were interest-free:*
> *Credit cards had yet to exist,*
> *So, there was no "over the limit" list.*

At the end of the school year at Fort Belvoir Elementary, Daddy announced we were moving to Kane Place, NE., in Washington, D.C. I cried to Mama that Daddy was moving again to punish me for not being his little girl because she stopped him from whipping me. Mama dismissed my complaint by yelling, "I told you Arthur Clay is your father, and that's final; are you calling me a liar?" I didn't say anything else.

Mama was angry, and I didn't want to cause her to have another heart attack. Additionally, I had learned those three words, along with that certain look she gave me, meant to shut up, or Mama would spank me.

My sixth address on Kane Place, NE, was a wooden two-bedroom house with a long porch. The one positive aspect of moving was that we didn't have to ride the bus from Fort Belvoir to visit Aunt Clo; I could walk to her house. My playmates had graduated to more advanced games: dominoes, Chinese checkers, and Monopoly.

George Washington Carver Elementary was my third elementary school. School staff tested me and skipped me to the third grade. As I had started school a year late, I felt like I was in the correct grade. On the flip side, having moved from school to school and skipping second grade, I missed some basic requirements, especially mathematics. My math skills remained poor throughout my life.

While attending Carver during the spring, I was running home from school one day and fell. I slid under a fence and tore my skin open over my left eye when I attempted to get up. One classmate, who was running with me, ran to my house and told Mama what had happened. When Mama got to me, someone who saw the accident took me and Mama to Walter Reed Hospital. A doctor cleaned the wound and glued it together; I did not have to get stitches. When we got home, Mama said, "Only my little Lou-Lou could have fallen under a fence." I cried because I was eight years old, and Mama continued to compare me to the comic strip character Little Lulu. I thought the little girl was funny-looking. Mama never called me that name again. It was okay to call me Lou, Lou-Lou, or Little Lou, but not Little Lulu.

> *Although I had to boo-hoo,*
> *Mama stopped calling me little Lou-Lou.*
> *When I was young, I laughed; it was cute,*
> *But it was time for the boot.*

Uncle David, Courtesy of David Jones, Jr.

Aunt Florence

Also in 1952, during the spring of fourth grade at Carver, Mama's youngest sister, Ollie Florence, her husband, David L. Jones, and their two-year-old daughter, Sylvia Jean (1950–2010), moved to Washington, D.C. They rented an apartment two blocks away from Aunt Clo and Uncle Tom. I didn't know how it came about,

Sylvia Jean

Me and Sylvia Jean

but I was excited to meet another aunt. She was eight years younger than Mama and nine years older than me. Coiffed bangs adorned her attractive face, and her tiny nose made me want to jiggle it. I saluted Uncle David in his blue Air Force uniform like I had seen soldiers salute Daddy.

During the summer school break of 1952, I went to Evington homecoming without Mama. We had not gone homecoming in 1950 or 1951 because of moving, and I wanted to go. I rode back and forth with Great-Aunt Louise's elder daughter and her husband. Mama and Aunt Clo stayed behind with her sister because she did not want to go. I don't know why. Perhaps it was because Aunt Florence was younger than three when her mother died, and an outside family took her in. She was unfamiliar with her Evington family. I stayed in Evington from June until the third weekend in August. In addition to seeing family, cousin Phyllis and I got to pal around the entire summer.

Upon my return from homecoming, I started fifth grade at Carver in the fall. I had completed the third and fourth grades at Carver. I could not believe we had stayed in one place for over two years. Mama told me the stork was bringing Uncle David and Aunt Florence another baby. The family was thrilled that there would soon be another family member.

When Aunt Florence's mother-in-law, Mother Jones, learned the news about the expected baby, she flew in from Chicago, Illinois, to live with her son and daughter-in-law to await the birth of her grandchild. It was customary for a family member to move in to help with a new baby before and after birth. The stocky, round-faced woman brought her 10-inch tabletop Muntz TV set. It was the first time I saw a television. The adult family and I were first exposed to wrestling by Mother Jones, who loved watching it. At almost ten, I could enjoy the sport with my older relatives; my little cousins were too young. We gathered around the small screen with Mother Jones and rooted for our favorite wrestlers. My favorite wrestler was Gorgeous George. He entered the ring in a robe with long blond hair and a "don't mess with me" macho strut. Mother Jones cooked tasty snacks to eat while watching wrestling. Additionally, she taught us family games to play when we weren't watching wrestling, like how many words we could find in a word she chose.

However, my fun and stability were short-lived; Daddy resumed punishing me, and that time we moved after school had started following the winter school break. Mama said nothing. Yet she fussed about most issues that she was not pleased with. I could not understand why Mama had protected me when Daddy whipped me, yet she had no problem with him moving me from place to place and school to school.

> *Again, Daddy moved mid-school year,*
> *And again, not because of his career.*
> *He moved to punish me.*
> *Why couldn't Mama see?*

SIX

SCHOOLS TO MY LOU
NUMBERS 4, 5, AND 6

My fourth, fifth, and sixth elementary "schools to my Lou" were: Burrville Elementary School in Washington, D.C.; Chattaroy Elementary School in West Virginia; and Fairmont Heights Elementary in Maryland, respectively. I completed the second half of the fifth grade at Burrville Elementary, the first half of the sixth grade at Chattaroy Elementary, and the second half of the sixth grade at Fairmont Heights. Those schools were also in the National Capital Region, including West Virginia. However, West Virginia was farther away than the schools I had attended, and Chattaroy Elementary was located in a coal-mining city.

Burrville Elementary was my fourth school in February. I had about four months left to complete the fifth grade. My seventh address was in an apartment building two streets from my aunts. Shortly after I started Burrville, the stork brought Aunt Florence

Poppa, Courtesy of David Jones, Jr.

Poppa

and Uncle David their second child in April 1953; they named him David Jr. Mother Jones said the baby acted like an old man and dubbed him Poppa. The family called him Poppa henceforth. Shortly after Poppa's birth, Aunt Clo announced the stork was bringing her another baby.

> *When we learned Auntie had a baby boy,*
> The family jumped for joy.
> Finally, a boy on the menu.
> Poppa was Mama's first nephew.

My memory of Burrville was that it was located in the middle of a steep hill, and as soon as I completed fifth grade, Daddy was deployed to the Korean Conflict for one year. The military would not allow Mama and I to accompany him because it was a war zone. Mama wrote her father and asked if we could stay with him. He welcomed us. He lived in Chattaroy, West Virginia, a coal mining town. I wanted to know why we couldn't stay with Aunt Clo. Mama dismissed my question and said we were going to West Virginia, adding, "And that's final!" I knew that meant I was not to say anything else. Looking back, Mama was probably seizing the opportunity for her father to spend time with me. He had never met me, and I was his firstborn grandchild. Further, Mama had not seen him since she left home at age sixteen.

Daddy, Mama, and I boarded a train to West Virginia in June of 1953. It was my first train ride, but I disliked everything about it. I didn't want to leave Bessie May, my other playmates, and my family behind, especially my baby cousin, Poppa. Thinking back, when Mama married and uprooted me from my family when I was 19 months old, I had to leave my first playmate, cousin Phyllis, behind. After about three years, she separated from him, and I lost my two playmates, who were her step-children. Mama left me with two different relatives while she regrouped. Each time she returned for me, I lost family and playmates, although the second time, I gained a dad and a nuclear family.

Then, after all of that, my new daddy beat me cruelly, and we began to move from place to place, resulting in the loss of classmates and playmates each time. Although the current move was a military deployment, Daddy had moved me from place to place for the past four years. I didn't want to connect with anyone anymore and feel the pain of leaving them behind again. I would keep my distance in the future. My connection button clicked off inside.

I had left my playmates at Aunt Clo's,
Bessie May, and her mother's clothes.
To avoid more loss and pain,
An introvert I became.

I drifted off to sleep. Mama woke me up as we approached Williamson, West Virginia, the business district for Chattaroy. It was around eight o'clock in the morning. Mama's father lived five miles across the railroad tracks. We caught a cab to Chattaroy, although we could have walked as people did; no one had automobiles.

When the cab arrived at Mama's father's house, John Reed Cooper, Jr., he greeted Daddy with a handshake, saying, "Glad to meet you, Sarge," and hugged Mama. Then he swooped me up and kissed me on the cheek as I giggled. I was surprised by his height of 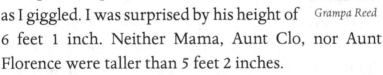 *Grampa Reed* 6 feet 1 inch. Neither Mama, Aunt Clo, nor Aunt Florence were taller than 5 feet 2 inches.

Hazel, Courtesy of Robert Childress

Grampa Reed had remarried. He introduced us to his much younger wife, Anniebell whose lengthy, flaming red-dyed hair accented her smooth vanilla-cream skin tone. She greeted us warmly, welcomed us, and introduced us to her 15-year-old daughter, Hazel.

After meeting my grandparents and Aunt Hazel, Gramma took Daddy and Mama to their room, and Grampa Reed put my suitcase in Aunt Hazel's room, where I would sleep. She had a radio and introduced me to Randy's Record Shop Radio Show out of Gallatin, Tennessee, on the AM radio dial, station WLAC. [5] Randy Wood played music for a mixed audience. Hazel could not access the station until 10 p.m. Static drowned the station out until daytime stations signed off. Aunt Hazel and I fell asleep listening to the radio. That was my introduction to radio and secular music, which includes rhythm and blues (R&B) tunes.

My eighth address was Chattaroy, West Virginia, a coal mining town in Mingo County worth a billion dollars and encircled by mountains. The day after we arrived, Grampa, Daddy, Mama, and I walked around Chattaroy. For the most part, it had a large store, a variety store, an elementary school, and a church. Grampa Reed was "The Company Man." He was the foreman of the coal mine, purchased his house from the mining company, and shopped at the company stores.

[5] WLAC –Radio, http://yodaslair.com/dumbozzle/wlac/wlacdex.html, assessed June 25, 2016.

From DC and headliners
To Chattaroy and coal miners:
The change was like night and day
And that was where I would stay?

Grampa Reed worked with John L. Lewis, President of the United Mine Workers of America. One of Lewis' duties was calling and ending coal mine strikes. Grampa Reed was responsible for preventing scabs from crossing the strike line. A strike took place a day or two after we arrived in Chattaroy. The twinkle in Grampa's eyes and how his body rocked from side to side as he walked showed that he was vibrant and in control. Several coal miners gathered at Grampa Reed's house and played cards during the strike until late at night. Grampa Reed did not allow me to go into the room where the men were gambling. I learned later that they were playing five-card stud poker. Daddy played with them until he left for Korea. I peeped into the room and saw Grampa Reed chewing tobacco and spitting in a can. I had never seen that before; it looked nasty. The strike lasted for a while.

Within a week, Daddy left for Korea. The week after that, the military delivered our personal belongings. Daddy and Mama left our furniture and most of our belongings in storage. Amongst our belongings was a 14-inch black and white tabletop television Daddy had put amongst the contents to surprise Mama. It was larger than Mother Jones' ten-inch tabletop predecessor. In 1953, no one else in Chattaroy had a TV. Neighbors gathered around the screen, drank soda pop, and ate snacks such as fried chicken, rabbit, and potato chips. The men drank beer. Like in Washington, D.C., with Mother Jones, everybody's favorite show was wrestling, including Aunt Hazel and me. The card players bet on the wrestlers. The losers bought chewing tobacco and beer.

Other programs on television instead of wrestling were: Make Room for Daddy, Your Show of Shows; Superman; Ed Sullivan; Roy Rogers; I Love Lucy; The Lone Ranger; Cisco Kid; Milton Berle; and What's My Line? However, only the women watched the other shows. The men only watched wrestling and played cards.

Because Chattaroy was between mountains, Grampa Reed constructed a makeshift antenna on the hill behind the house for better reception. At the end of the wrestling matches, our parents made Aunt Hazel and me clean up the living room. We didn't like that chore. We grumbled, "Why can't the grownups clean up behind themselves?"

> *Neighbors loved the television screen,*
> *Chewing tobacco, food, and caffeine.*
> *Wrestling was the favored program;*
> *Everyone enjoyed the bam and slam.*

Between playing cards and wrestling, Grampa Reed assembled a bicycle for me from bicycles under his porch that belonged to his children years ago. He bought two new tires. My first two-wheel bike was cool: red and silver with a spotlight, bell to ring, and front and rear fenders. Mama told Grampa Reed that she did not want me to ride the bike and recounted how riding my trike down 49th Street in Washington, DC, more than three years ago had scared her. Grampa Reed told her it was foolish for her to continue to deprive me of riding a bike because of something that happened that long ago. Grampa Reed gave me a quick bike lesson and sent me on my way.

In addition to riding my bike, the neighborhood kids also taught me how to shoot marbles. I won a quart jar full of beautiful, colorful marbles. They also taught me to play a different game of hide and seek. At Aunt Clo's, everyone hid alone, and the seeker counted to ten and sought to find those who had hidden. In Chattaroy, a boy and a girl hid together, and nobody searched for anybody. The boy I hid with kissed me. It was my first kiss. His lips on mine made me anxious and nervous. If Mama found out, she would whip me. I never told Mama, and I never played that game again. However, I did think about the kiss and how it made me feel tingly.

While playing games and having fun, near the end of summer, Mama's youngest brother, Charles Marshall

Cooper, came home from the mental hospital for a visit. His father had placed him in the mental hospital before his mother passed away in 1936. Uncle Charles was in his mid-twenties and childlike. Grampa explained that Dr. Walter Freeman, the father of lobotomy, had performed a lobotomy on my good-looking, muscular uncle last year, which left him in a vegetative state. Uncle Charles was home for about a week when someone discovered him switching the railroad tracks between Chattaroy and Williamson and informed the sheriff's office. Grampa Reed had to return him to the hospital; the lobotomy had failed.

After Uncle Charles' return to the hospital, it was time for me to begin sixth grade at Chattaroy Elementary. It was a one-room schoolhouse. I don't remember how many students were in the class, but there were more girls than boys. At the sound of the school bell, we lined up and marched in daily. When we got inside, we stood and recited the names of the 48 states and their capitals, beginning with Washington State, as they appeared on the map. Then, we recited the names of the United States presidents and vice presidents in the order they served. Students earned a lash on whuppin' days for every incorrect recital and every incorrect response to a question on a pop quiz or scheduled exam. Corporal punishment was legal in West Virginia.

I retained a few of the daily recitals
Of the presidents and state capitals.
However, it failed to fulfill the intention
That repetition equaled retention.

On whuppin' days, the teacher sent two boys to get three switches from a dogwood tree. Those branches were strong. The boys always volunteered to take the licks for the girls; they were gentlemen. The instructor made the boys lie across a chair in the center of the classroom. She then aimed and delivered a powerful wallop. It gave me flashbacks to the time Daddy beat me at age six.

The same month school started, Great-Uncle Herb Whiteside, Gramma Bell's brother, came to live with his sister and brother-in-law. He put the "P" in personality and the "G" in good looks and generosity. He went to the variety store and told the storeowner to allow me to spend up to $30 biweekly, and he would pay the bill. I bought games, toys, sweets, and anything else I wished. I was rich!

Herb Whiteside

On Christmas Eve during school break, I was attempting to drift off to sleep so Santa could come, and Aunt Hazel poked fun at me. She remarked, "There's no Santa; stay awake, and you'll see." I didn't believe her, but I couldn't fall asleep. In the still of the night,

I heard the door open. It was Mama checking to see if I had gone to sleep. I pretended to be asleep. When she closed the door, I tiptoed, peeped through the key-hole, and saw Mama putting love under the tree. Aunt Hazel had told me the truth. Mama was Santa. In the morning, Mama had put a 23-inch walking doll and clothing under the tree. I informed Mama that Aunt Hazel had told me there was no Santa. Mama was upset. She told her that it was not her place to tell me. She said Aunt Hazel knew better because she was in high school and I was in elementary school. I felt sad for Mama; however, it could not be undone. I named my doll Sonya.

> *During my Chattaroy stay,*
> *Aunt Hazel ruined my Xmas Day.*
> *She told me that Santa was a gag;*
> *The cat was out of the bag.*

Although Aunt Hazel's ruining my Christmas had nothing to do with it, Mama decided to leave Chattaroy at the beginning of the New Year. Aunt Clo had writ-ten Mama the week of Christmas to tell her that their remaining siblings had migrated to Washington, D.C., and that she had given birth to another baby girl in November. Mama had informed me about her other siblings, and I was anxious to meet them. I had only met Aunt Clo, Aunt Florence, and Uncle Charles. Besides,

I would see my playmates and Bessie May sooner than anticipated.

We caught a train to Washington, D.C., the first week of January. I would miss Grampa Reed, Great-Uncle Herb, my $30 biweekly spending account, riding my bike, and shooting marbles. I left my Christmas doll, Sonya, Mama left our television, and everything else we couldn't fit into one large suitcase and one small one. She carried the large one, and I lugged the small bag. However, as my connection button had clicked off on the way to West Virginia, leaving playmates behind again was less painful. I never saw Uncle Charles, Great-Uncle Herb, Gramma Anniebell, or Aunt Hazel again, although I spoke to Aunt Hazel on the phone a few times years later. Hazel Virginia Childress passed away on June 5, 2024.

> *A letter from Aunt Clo*
> *Prompted Mama to go.*
> *We returned to DC*
> *To meet more family.*

On the train, Mama told me we were returning to D.C. so that I could meet her other three siblings: John Reed 'Buster' Cooper, Jr., James Willie "Bill" Cooper, and Marjorie Marie "Margie" Cooper (I had met Uncle Charles, Aunt Clo, and Aunt Florence). Mama had told me before, but she reiterated that three of her siblings had passed away, two as teenagers: Clara Anderson, Maggie Elizabeth, and her youngest sister, Margaret Ann, at one day old. Maggie Elizabeth had left the family who was raising her as a teenager and died somewhere singing on the road. Mama did not know when, where, or exactly how it happened. I felt sad that I would never know three of my aunts.

Mamas elder brother, John Reed "Buster" Cooper, Jr., a warm-hearted southpaw with smiling eyes, picked

Uncle Buster

Aunt Pauline

us up at Union Train Station in Washington, D.C. There was no Amtrak. Washington, D.C., was bright compared to the dark coalmine town I had lived in for the past six months. Uncle Buster was Mama's elder brother; he was six years older. He took us to his home. His wife's name was Pauline (1928–1992). Her

Barbara

Doll

tiny waistline and itty-bitty feet stood out. Uncle Buster and Aunt Pauline called each other "babe." They had two children then. Aunt Pauline led Mama to her daughter Margaret's room, called "Doll" (1950–2009), where she would sleep, and directed me to her older daughter Barbara's room, where I would sleep. I learned Barbara was born five months before Aunt Clo's twins, making her my next oldest cousin instead of the twins. Uncle Buster told Mama he had been living in North Carolina, where he met his wife.

After Mama and I parked our suitcases, Uncle Buster drove all of us to their sister Marjorie Marie's and her

Uncle Jesse

Aunt Margie

husband Jesse Reed DeVaughn's house (1928–1982). Mama and Auntie embraced, and they cried. Like her baby sister, Florence, an outside family raised Aunt Margie after her mother died; she was almost seven. Aunt Margie was four years younger than

Gwendolyn

Horace

Mama. Mama and her sisters were under 5 feet 2 inches. Of my three aunts, I looked more like Aunt Margie. They had two children then: Gwendolyn Deloris (1950–2004) and Horace Jesse (1952–2024). Uncle Jesse took time to meet us, but the handsome, dapperly dressed man was on the way out when we arrived. Although Grampa Reed and Uncle Jesse had the same middle names, I found no relationship.

We left and drove to Aunt Florence's, where I met natural curly-haired James Willie "Bill" Cooper. Uncle Bill was 14 months older than Mama. They favored most of the siblings. Buleah, his cute, petite wife, greeted us cheerfully. Her ample bosom was the first to catch the eye. They did not have children. Unfortunately, I could not locate a picture of Uncle Bill or Aunt Buleah. I looked around for Mother Jones, and she was not present. Aunt Florence said she had returned to Chicago after Christmas. Her grandson, Poppa, had turned eight months old, and she had been in Washington, D.C., since before his birth. She left her television behind for her son and daughter-in-law. I never saw Mother Jones again.

Next, everyone walked down the street to Aunt Clo's house, and Mama and I met Aunt Clo's newborn

daughter, Brenda Kaye. She was six weeks old and five years younger than her twin sisters. Her thick, black hair was what

Brenda Kay I remembered. She slept the en- *Brenda Kay*

tire time we were there. Uncle Tom served us something to eat and drink.

After meeting Aunt Margie, two uncles, and five additional cousins, I asked Mama if I could visit Bessie May. She told me I could. When I got to Bessie May's and knocked on her door, the person who answered told me the previous renters had moved. Bessie May and her mother had vanished. I cried. I saw a few of my other playmates, but no one had a forwarding address for Bessie May. I never saw my best friend again; the losses from moving were piling up.

Where did they flee?
Our friendship wasn't meant to be.
Why did it turn out that way?
I never forgot Bessie May.

After I returned from Bessie May's, Uncle Buster drove us back to his house. The next day, Barbara and I contracted chickenpox. We were quarantined for ten days. No other family member got chickenpox. When our pox had run its course, Mama turned her attention to finding a place for us to live so she could enroll me in school to complete sixth grade. Someone told Uncle Buster about a vacancy a few miles from where he lived. He drove Mama to see it. She liked it, and we moved in the next day. It was a house we shared with the owner. Mama and I had separate rooms. My ninth abode was in Fairmount Heights, Maryland. Aunt Florence, Aunt Clo, and Uncle Buster were within walking distance. It was a long walk to Uncle Buster's, but we saw Aunts Clo and Florence almost daily. Uncle Bill and Aunt Margie lived across town.

Although Uncle Bill did not live nearby, he caught the bus and visited us often. Mama had bought an ordinary table with a glass top for her room. Uncle Bill painted bright, colorful flowers on the underside of the glass, making the ordinary table a conversation piece. He was an artist. I never knew what happened to the table, and I don't remember seeing anything else Uncle Bill painted. He also brought Mama a cocker spaniel puppy that he had potty trained. I enjoyed having a pet to walk with, play with, and cuddle with. Each time Uncle Bill came, we walked to the store, and he bought me goodies. He was attentive, nice, and glad to meet his sister Rene's daughter. We spent a lot of time together. I looked forward to Uncle Bill's visits.

> *The puppy was a golden male.*
> *He had curly ears and a nubby tail.*
> *Since the canine was a plump puppy,*
> *Mama named him Chubby.*

Mama enrolled me in Fairmont Heights Elementary School immediately, and I finished sixth grade in four months. It was the sixth elementary school I attended. In addition to Fairmont Heights Elementary, I attended three elementary schools in Washington, D.C., one in Virginia, and one in West Virginia. Many kids lived in the same neighborhood and attended the same elementary school from beginning to end. I regret not attending a single elementary school where I could have spent my elementary school years with the same classmates and friends from the neighborhood.

While completing elementary school, we visited our families, and they visited us. During the summer, we continued to unite with our families. No one had a phone, but we located each other; we all ended up at the same family member's house. At the end of the summer, Aunt Florence and Aunt Margie announced that they were expecting another baby next year.

SEVEN

SCHOOLS TO MY LOU
NUMBERS 7, 8, AND 9

My seventh, eighth, and ninth "schools to my Lou" were: Fairmont Heights High School in Maryland; Union Elementary School in Virginia; and A.G. Richardson High School in Virginia. I completed the first half of the seventh grade at Fairmont Heights High School, the second half of the seventh grade at Union Elementary, and half of the eighth grade at A.G. Richardson. The schools in Virginia were between 75 and 100 miles from Washington, D.C.

In September, I began the seventh grade at Fairmont Heights High School. It was also my seventh school. I

met two sisters who were also neighbors. Loretta, on the right side of the picture, was my age and attended Fairmont Heights High. I don't remember what her sister's name was. The other individual I met was Tommy Broadwater, the

Me, Loretta and her Sister

most popular boy at Fairmont Heights High. He went on to become a Maryland state senator and an entrepreneur. After attending school for about a month, Mama received a letter from Daddy telling her he would be home before Christmas.

Senator Broadwater and me

When Daddy returned from Korea, the military assigned him to Fort A.P. Hill in Virginia, his second military relocation. Between Christmas and New Year's school breaks, we moved to Bowling Green, Virginia, my tenth address. It was close to where Daddy was stationed. We lived in a three-bedroom house in a quiet bedroom community, where the military delivered our household items from storage that we had not taken to West Virginia. We left Chubby with the landlord; she loved him. Dogs were not allowed.

> *While I had lost many human friends,*
> *That was my first furry friendship to end.*
> *With my pet, I had been less lonely;*
> *Now I had to leave Chubby.*

Mama received letters from Aunt Florence and Aunt Margie in Bowling Green. Aunt Florence and Uncle David had delivered a baby girl in February, and they were moving to Denver, Colorado. Their son, Poppa, had contracted a severe case of asthma. He had to live in a dry climate. Aunt Florence also informed Mama that Uncle Bill and Aunt Beulah had separated, and he had moved in with Uncle Buster and their family.

Aunt Margie wrote that she and Uncle Jesse Reed delivered a baby boy in January, and they were moving to Philadelphia, Pennsylvania, near her husband's family. Two of my three aunts and their families were moving miles away. I didn't get to see my two new first cousins.

> Two aunts and uncles were moving away.
> Unfortunately, they couldn't stay.
> Our families were splitting,
> And togetherness was shattering.

Union Elementary was my eighth school, where I completed seventh grade. My memory of Union was taking piano lessons, playing basketball, and making group letter formations like marching bands. A neighbor also taught me piano lessons for five of the six months we were in Bowling Green. When school ended in the summer, we moved to Pendleton, Virginia, near Louisa. It was about 45 miles from Bowling Green. As a young person, I never learned to play the piano again.

My 11th address in Pendleton, Virginia, was a single-family brick house about a quarter of a mile from the road. Daddy bought us a radio instead of another television. Mama and I listened to The Shadow on the radio on Wednesday evenings and recited the catchphrase in unison when the program came on: "Who knows what evil lurks in the hearts of men? The Shadow knows!"

Great Aunt Dorothy's son, Jimmy, lived five miles from Pendleton in Louisa. We had not seen him since I left his mother's house at age six. He gave us one of his three dogs, a black male two-year-old Labrador Retriever named Diamond, because of a white patch in the center of his head in the shape of a diamond. We fell in love with him, and he became a part of our family.

In the fall, my ninth school to complete eighth grade in Pendleton was A.G. Richardson High School. I had to catch the school bus. Diamond walked with me to the road and met me in the evening. I recall a handsome high school student at Richardson named Henry who drove the bus. I was the only student who boarded the bus in Pendleton. I don't remember much more about Richardson High School, where I completed the first half of the eighth grade.

Grampa Reed visited us in Pendleton and stayed for about two months. He informed us that Gramma Bell and Aunt Hazel had left him after Hazel graduated from high school. Grampa and I walked up to the road on Saturdays; it was our time together. He continued to enjoy the television we left in West Virginia but was no longer the only one to own a television in Chattaroy. One piece of advice that Grampa Reed gave me was,

"Learn to pick your battles." He told me I would learn what it meant when I grew up.

While Grampa was visiting, Uncle Buster drove down several times on weekends to visit his father. Each time he came, he let me steer his car. As my legs were too short to reach the brake and gas pedals, I sat on his lap, and he operated them while I turned the steering wheel. I drove around and around the house and learned to steer his car. I would be able to drive as soon as my legs grew.

When Grampa Reed was ready to return home, Daddy drove him to Washington, D.C., to visit his other children and grandchildren. Mama and I rode along. Although Aunts Margie and Florence had left D.C., Grampa Reed told us they had visited him in West Virginia. Grampa was ready to return home before Christmas, although we tried to get him to stay longer. He had spent time with his family and wanted to go home. It was the last time I saw Grampa vibrant and healthy.

Not long after Grampa Reed left, the military transferred Daddy back to Fort Belvoir during my winter school break. Before the Korean deployment, Daddy had been a cook at Fort Belvoir for several years; I guess they wanted him back. This was the fourth and final move that the military ordered. They all resulted from the Korean deployment. Mama returned Diamond to cousin Jimmy, as dogs would not be allowed. I had no human friends save for Mama, and I lost another furry friend. For the fifth time, I would attend another school to finish the second half of a grade; it had become commonplace.

The four moves on the military's radar —
Were WV, two cities in VA, and Ft. Belvoir.
At least those moves weren't to punish me.
Gratefully, Fort Belvoir was closer to family.

SCHOOLS TO MY LOU
NUMBERS 10, 11, AND 12

My tenth, eleventh, and twelfths "schools to my Lou" were: Luther Jackson High School in Merrifield, Virginia, Gillespie Junior High in Philadelphia, Pennsylvania, and Langley Junior High in Washington, D.C. I completed eighth grade at Luther Jackson High School, one week of the ninth grade at Gillespie Junior High in Philadelphia, and completed Junior High in Washington, D.C. at Langley Junior High.

At Fort Belvoir, move number 12, where I attended Luther Jackson High School, I met a thirteen-year-old girl my age named Jessie, who taught me to smoke cigarettes and told me to lift them from Mama's pack. Our fathers smoked Camels that didn't have a filter; they were too strong. Our mothers, in contrast, smoked Winston cigarettes with a filter on the tip. We rode the school bus together, and one day, Jessie blurted out the well-known Winston cigarette slogan. The students loved it and laughed haughtily. The US Supreme Court had integrated schools two years earlier, with the passage of Brown v. Board of Education in May 1954. However, implementation was slow. The bus passed by white schools that were still segregated.

An unforeseen event occurred at Fort Belvoir. Aunt Margie and Uncle Jesse Reed asked my parents to raise

their 14-month-old son, Terry Michael. My parents said yes. He was the baby born when we lived in Bowling Green. They had delivered a fourth child, and the oldest was only five; they needed help. We drove to

Terry,
Courtesy
of Terry
Devaughn

Terry,
Courtesy
of Terry
Devaughn

Philadelphia to bring Terry back. The 35-pound, jolly, cherubic boy was mild-mannered as long as Mama kept a milk bottle in his pocket. I loved having a brother. We called him Michael, but later on, as everyone else called him Terry, we did too.

One day, I took Terry outside to play. Before I knew it, he disappeared. We joined the military police to search for him. Within 30 minutes, we found him eating coal inside a coal bin. When Mama grabbed him up, he kicked, screamed, and had a tantrum. He wanted to continue eating coal. Unfortunately, the military police involvement exposed that Terry was not Daddy's dependent. We had to vacate Fort Belvoir.

The military allowed us to stay until I completed my school year.

> *Terry wasn't Daddy's dependent;*
> *The rule couldn't be bent:*
> *Our stay was only extended*
> *Until my school year ended.*

We moved from Fort Belvoir to 64 T Street, NW, in Washington, D.C., in June 1956. My Aunt Clo had told

my parents about a vacant basement apartment in the same house where she lived. (I took the picture in 2023; the only change was the painted door, brick, and the black iron fence next to the basement

64 T Street, NW

entrance.) Near the end of a long hallway were two bedrooms separated by a bathroom, and there was a rear exit door. I slept on a rollaway cot in the hallway closer to the front entrance, living room, and kitchen, and that muffled Daddy's snoring. Terry slept in the other bedroom that housed mine and his clothing. I was 13, and T Street was my 13th move.

When Daddy and his helpers had unloaded the U-Hall truck, Mama and I discovered a television in one of the boxes. He surprised Mama again. However, unlike the 14-inch tabletop black and white Muntz television in West Virginia, it was a 21-inch floor model Motorola color television. It had four wooden legs and a mahogany cabinet. In 1956, color television was still making its way into mainstream American homes. Mama and I were elated. Most of the programming was:

> Gunsmoke, Amos 'n' Andy; Alfred Hitchcock; the Arthur Godfrey Show; the $64,000 Question; the Jack Benny Show; the Ed Sullivan Show; Lassie; Jackie Gleason; the George Burns and Gracie Allen Show; the Art Linkletter Show; Wyatt Earp; Walter Cronkite; baseball, and wrestling.

Daddy loved baseball and watched it on television for hours with a camel cigarette dangling from his lips. The Brooklyn Dodgers were his favorite team because they broke the segregation barrier with Jackie Robinson in 1947. Daddy also watched the Jack Benny Show. Age 39 was the age that he and Daddy chose to remain. Otherwise, Daddy hadn't been interested in television. Mama and I watched most of the other programs. However, we no longer watched wrestling. We had learned it was fake and lost interest in watching it. In addition to a radio and television, Daddy had the Chesapeake and Potomac (C&P) Telephone Company install our first telephone. We had not used a phone since we left Seaton Place, NW, in 1949, where we used the landlady's.

On T Street, vendors drove horse-drawn wagons and sold various food items, as they had at Fort Belvoir. However, merchants soon began selling housewares door-to-door from their cars. The payment system remained the same—buy now and pay a dollar or two weekly. Mama and the vendor tallied their books together each week as she had with the vendors at Fort Belvoir. Mama added items weekly to her bill.

In a couple of weeks, after Mama and I had unpacked and placed everything on T Street, we rode the bus to Uncle Buster's and Aunt Pauline's in early July. They had moved to Kentland, Maryland. Mama dropped me off and left for a while. Aunt Pauline allowed me to play outdoors. Uncle Buster was at work. I ran inside for a drink of water, and Auntie made me stay inside. She

Aunt Pauline and Uncle Buster, Courtesy of Barbara Banks

didn't tell me why, and I wondered what I had done. Mama returned, and Aunt Pauline whispered in her ear. Mama went back out. When she returned, she took me into the bathroom and showed me how to use the feminine protection she had purchased. Mama told me Aunt Pauline saw blood on my dress. Mama instructed: "Keep your pocketbook shut, and you won't get pregnant." Those nine words were the extent of my sex education.

The topic of sex was taboo;
It was something not to do.
There was no discussion
About any repercussions.

In early August, Mama, Terry, and I boarded a bus to Philadelphia, Pennsylvania, to visit Aunt Margie,

Terry's birth mother. In keeping with custom, Mama decided to go and help her sister out, who now had three small children, excluding Terry. The baby,

Mama and Aunt Margie

Ronnie, Courtesy of Ronnie Devaughn

Ronnie, was four months old. Mama intended to stay until December of my ninth-grade school year. Daddy agreed. Mama also wanted Terry to have the opportunity to play with his siblings.

Gillespie Junior High, my eleventh school, was where I began ninth grade in Philadelphia in September. There were gangs in Philly. Young people had the choice of joining a gang in Washington, D.C.; they were forced into gangs in Philadelphia. At the beginning of school, gang fights occurred in front of Gillespie almost every day. Mama had intended to stay longer, but she feared for my life. Auntie understood. We returned to Washington, D.C., the second week of school.

Back home to Washington, D.C., I joined the role at Langley Junior High on September 24, 1956. That was my 12th school. The principal of Langley, Valerie Chase, had a strict dress code. She did not allow makeup, grown-up-looking dresses, or high-heeled shoes. Behind her back, students called her "Bulldog Chase."

Because Principal Chase was strict, Mama allowed me to begin listening to the R&B and doo-wop music on the radio that Aunt Hazel introduced me to in West Virginia. She also bought me a record player. Before and after that time, Mama had only allowed me to listen to gospel music. The one radio station in Washington, D.C., that played Negro R&B and doo-wop music was WOOK, 1340 on the AM radio dial. I used my allowance to buy hit records at the Waxi-Maxi record store. Initially, I only purchased 45 records. The cost of a 45-vinyl record was less than a dollar.

Waxi-Maxi's record store was one street over from the historic Howard Theater, where Negroes attended to see performers. It was a part of the Chitlin' Circuit, the name given to venues where Negros had to perform during the era of racial segregation. I dreamed of going to the Howard Theater to see the entertainers I heard on the radio and records; Mama would not permit me to go.

While at Langley Junior High,
Radio was AM and Hi-Fi:
Records were made of vinyl,
And 45s used a record spindle.

As I could not go to see the R&B and doo-wop singers perform at the Howard Theater, I imagined how they looked as I sang along with them on the radio and my record player. I used a tablespoon for my microphone. I persisted in asking Mama if I could go to the Howard, hoping each time that she would say yes. By the way, comedians like Clay Tyson, Moms Mabley, and Redd Fox also appeared at the Howard. I also wanted to see them.

During this time, Mama and I were sitting on the stoop one day, and two of Mama's previous church members, Deacon and Deaconess Edward "Ed" and Dorothy "Dot" Bolling, came walking by. The Bollings and Mama struck up a conversation. Their place of worship,

Deaconess Dot Mt. Pleasant Baptist Church, where Mama had stopped attending, had relocated two blocks down the street on Rhode Island Avenue, NW. They tried to convince Mama to reinstate her church membership. Mama suggested that they take me to church instead. They did, and eventually became my godparents. Ed also became a father figure; I welcomed that.

Ed and Dot began taking me to Bible study and church. I loved going to church and hearing live gospel singing again. In March 1957, at age 14, Pastor Robert Anderson baptized me at Mt. Pleasant Baptist Church. Ed was what I thought a dad should be. He guided me and showed me love. Then, within two months of my baptism, Ed went to claim his mansion in Heaven. I didn't know he was ill. It was my first experience with death and a tremendous loss. He was the father I wished I had. Ed was in my life briefly, and then he was gone. Although my godmother was nice and caring, she could not help me; I needed a father figure. I became disillusioned and strayed away from church.

Not long after Ed's death, Mama and I found a mixed boxer puppy on our steps. The butterscotch-brown dog was three to four months old. Mama gave him some food and bathed him. He became a part of our family. She named him Butch. I was overjoyed at having another dog. There was no leash law. Butch roamed free and came home when he wanted to eat, drink, sleep, or when we called him.

Also, about that time, Mama, Aunt Clo, and I started going to bingo. However, Mama only took me when Aunt Clo did not go because I was the babysitter for Terry and Aunt Clo's three girls when she went. The twins were the oldest at eight, and I was 14. The Catholic Church awarded prizes to winners instead of money. I was lucky; I won lots of prizes. Admission was two dollars. Over the years, bingo changed from awarding prizes to paying money to winners. The cost of admission greatly increased.

> *That was the beginning of bingo;*
> *For Mama, me, and Aunt Clo:*
> *It cost two dollars to play;*
> *A fraction of the cost today.*

Time passed while playing bingo, studying, babysitting, and listening to records for the mostly, and Principal Chase was planning our junior high graduation. Instead of a prom, she decided on a dance in the gymnasium, with music different from what we students danced to. The boys were on one side of the room and the girls on the other. We mostly giggled at the music being played and our awareness of the differences between boys and girls; some had developed more than others.

The next day, a photographer took our group graduation picture. I wore a crinoline under my dress so I didn't look skinny.

Langley Graduation photo

Suppose Column

Our final 1957 Langley Light newspaper was printed on the reverse of our graduation pictures. In our newspaper, there was a "Suppose Column."

Regarding me, the writer wrote: Suppose "Louise were Mud instead of Clay." (5th line from the top). As you can see, the writers of the Langley Light were deep thinkers.

Following graduation, Mama had a family get-together to celebrate my completion of junior high school. Aunt Clo, Uncle Buster, Aunt Pauline, and their families, along with Uncle Bill, came and bought gifts. I was surprised that Mama also invited cousin Gladys, who was present the day I was born. I had not seen much of her over the years. I played

Cousin Gladys

my records, and we danced. The highlight of the get-together was Mama doing a dance called 'Truckin,' similar to the Camel Walk, a dance popularized by James Brown in the 1960s. I was shocked to see her dancing. Mama admitted that she had danced in school despite her doctor's warning against strenuous activity because of her heart condition.

The summer of my graduation from Langley Junior High, I began hanging out at the stage door of the

Roy Hamilton's Autograph

Howard Theater, where entertainers arrived and left. The first entertainer I met was Roy Hamilton. I loved his singing and had purchased his latest hit, "You'll Never Walk Alone." Hamilton was polite, and I enjoyed talking to him. His deep dimples and playful smile made me feel at ease. I told him I was interested in being a singer, too. He said, "If you're serious, I will arrange an audition with my manager, Bill Cook." He told me that Bill Cook was a deejay in New Jersey and a songwriter who got a record deal for him. He introduced me to Bill Cooke. I told them I had to ask my mother first and I would come back tomorrow.

Bill Cook's autograph

I ran home to ask Mama if I could audition and learned that she had talked to Aunt Florence and had promised to send me to Denver, Colorado, for two weeks. I was conflicted. I wanted to meet their youngest daughter, who had been born while we were living in Bowling Green, but I had not gotten the opportunity to see her. I missed my family. At the same time, I wanted to attend the audition. Whatever my choice, it did not matter; Mama had made it for me. However, she made my train ride to Denver enjoyable by packing my favorite brown bag lunch:

> *Potato Salad and Apple pie;*
> *The best beneath the sky:*
> *Fried chicken and a hambone;*
> *I ate off and on until it was gone.*

My aunt and uncle picked me up at the train station, and I met my two-year-old cousin, Donna Marie, for the first time. She had a round face like her grandmother, Mother Jones. I was surprised at how much Poppa and

Sylvia Jean had grown in two years. Sylvia Jean remembered me, but Poppa was too young when he left D.C. to remember me. I stayed for two weeks and returned home.

Donna Marie   Roy Hamilton and Bill Cook had moved on from the Howard Theater, and I never saw them again.

The week I came home from Denver, Colorado, I met a girl named Rita. She was the stepdaughter of our landlord, who came from time to time to inspect his property and sometimes brought her with him. Her wide hips and big legs were attractive. We talked and liked each other immediately. Before

Rita

long, her dad allowed her to sleep over on occasion. We were the same age. In a couple of months, Mama permitted Rita and me to have a party. I had all the latest records. Blue lights in the basement were popular in the 1950s, so Rita and I purchased a blue light with our allowances to give the basement a warm glow. We laughed at how the blue light made lint visible on clothing. Word spread about the party, and many teens came. We didn't know most of them. They danced inside and outside in the entryway. Mama stayed in her room down the hallway and let us have fun until it got rowdy. Then she came and stopped the music. It was our first and last blue lights in the basement party.

Next, I met Mary Jane, Sudie, Joyce, and Almeta. Mary was called "Little Mary" because she and a giant goose would stand toe to toe height-wise. Joyce favored J. C.

Hayward, who became a news anchor for WUSA9 in 1972. Sudie's red hair and freckles were eye-catching and unique for a Negro. Her red hair contrasted with Joyce's black hair. Muscular and re-

Mary

served, Mary's sister, Almeta, was older than the rest of us. Although Joyce lived within walking distance and we were in the same grade, she lived in a different school zone and could not go to the same

Sudie, Courtesy of Clarence Jones

school we attended. Sudie and Mary were one year ahead of me, but we attended the same high school in the fall. Almeta had either completed high school or dropped out. I never knew which. Mary and I grav-

Joyce

itated toward one another, and my connection button inside turned back on. As time passed, I compared Mary to Huckleberry Finn. Both of them were smart, loved to laugh, had an easygoing personality, and were positive-minded. Considering she was female, I added an "a" for feminine gender, and she became my "Huckleberrya" friend, although I called her Mary.

Mary was a Godsend.
We were a perfect blend.
She became my "Huckleberrya" friend.
She had been waiting around the bend.

My new friends told me about the Caravan Ballroom at Ninth and V Streets, NW, where teenagers near and far gathered on Sunday nights to dance and socialize in a large room. Admission was 25 cents. I joined my new friends in walking to the caravan the next Sunday to dance. The fast dance was called hand dancing, and the slow dance was the rub or grind. I did not like to dance fast; I liked slow dancing. Sudie and one of her friends visited me one Saturday, and they held out a hand, asking Daddy for a quarter to go to the caravan the next day. He gave each of them a quarter, saw my outstretched hand, and smirked, "I ain't got no more money." Daddy and I had related mostly via Mama since he beat me at age six; I should have known better than to ask him for anything. As I had spent my allowance on records, Mama came to my rescue and gave me a quarter to go to the caravan.

My next fun activity with my newfound friends was a five-mile walk, one way, to the Ringling Brothers and Barnum and Bailey Carnival at 34th and Benning Roads, NE. The fun house, haunted house, freaks of nature, and carnival rides were exciting, and the cotton candy and caramel apples were delicious. The girls tried to win prizes by throwing balls into baskets or holes. The boys shot rifles at targets and played the bell-and-hammer game to win stuffed toys for their sweethearts. Everyone threw pennies and tried to win carnival dishes for our parents.

While walking home from the carnival, Joyce told me she liked to sing. She began to come to my house, and we sang along with records. One day, Joyce asked me to join the Marteen Club, where teens danced on Friday nights. Joyce loved to dance. However, the Marteen Club was a part of St. Martin's Catholic Church, and one had to be a member of the church to join the club. We completed the requirements, were baptized, and joined the Marteen Club. It was located in the church gymnasium, and above one of the basketball hoops was a small area where a priest sat and chaperoned. If we danced too close on a slow tune, he yelled, "Immoral dancing; you know who you are." I liked to slow dance, so I left the church and the club before long. Joyce remained. We continued to sing together.

After a fun-filled summer with my new friends, Mama, Terry, and I went to the 1957 Evington homecoming for most of August. Mama wanted Terry to meet his great-aunts and other family members. Daddy could not get off work. I looked for Cousin Phyllis and asked if anyone had seen her. I learned she had passed away at age 12 from diabetes complications (1942–1954). The last time I saw my first playmate was when I spent the summer in Evington in 1952. Having moved several times after the 1952 Evington homecoming, we did not attend again until 1957; we had not heard the news. I was sorrowful. Not seeing Patricia again was unimaginable. For some reason, we had not written to one another over the years; we waited to communicate and interact during homecoming. Her dark, bright eyes, which twinkled with the innocence of a lovely, young Southern girl, have lived on in my memory.

> *Born the same year, Phyllis was gone.*
> *Never to see her again when I came home.*
> *Sweet Southern girl, a bird of paradise;*
> *Having known her was like sugar and spice.*

Unfortunately, in addition to learning of Phyllis's death, the 1957 Evington homecoming was the final one for my great aunts, as they were ailing and unable to continue preparing for homecomings. It was time for the younger generation to step up, but none did. The family reunions kept our family history and culture alive. It enabled us to see each other and our elders in our hometown. We also got to see newborns. The reunions ended for the families of Great-Aunts Louise and Gladys in the summer of 1957; I was 14 years old.

NINE

SCHOOLS TO MY LOU
NUMBERS 13, AND 14

My thirteenth and fourteenth "schools to my Lou" were McKinley Technical High School (Tech) in Washington, D.C., and Luther Jackson High school in Merrifield, Virginia. I completed the tenth through half of the twelfth grades at Tech, and the final half (actually about three months) of the twelfth grade at Luther Jackson High School.

My sophomore year began at McKinley Technical High School (Tech) in September 1957. It was school number 13. Tech was a school on a hill. Students walked up the 30-something steps every day to enter the school. My tenth-grade algebra teacher polled the class and found that none of his students planned to go to college; therefore, he considered teaching us algebra a waste of time. He discussed current events

McKinley Tech (The picture was taken in 2023. The steps were the same steps).

and sports the entire year and gave us a passing grade. I had missed the basic building blocks of math while moving; thus, his decision was fine with me. Besides, my goals were to be married, have a family, and work as a secretary in the federal government.

> *Tech was called the thrill upon the hill;*
> *It was not a school that was run of the mill:*
> *Our football team was extraordinary,*
> *And our choir sang as sweet as a canary.*

Most sophomores at Tech had fully developed physically. I was an exception and thought boys weren't interested in me. Then one evening, not long after school started, Butch and I were sitting on the steps, and a soldier passing by stopped to say hello. He wore an Army khaki uniform with a foldable garrison cap, like Daddy's non-formal uniform. He introduced himself as Boyd. We talked, and he said he was a career soldier. I told him my name and that my dad was also a career soldier. He stopped by daily over the next two weeks and eventually became my first boyfriend.

Boyd invited me to dinner at his mother's house for Thanksgiving. The evening was enjoyable until Boyd excused himself to go to the bathroom, and his mother told me, in confidence, that her son was impersonating a soldier. Boyd returned to the table, and I was jittery. I told him I was ready to go home. He walked me to my door, and I broke up with him. He hung his head and withdrew without a word. He must have guessed that his mother had exposed him. I never saw him again.

My breakup with my first boyfriend softened Mama's heart about the Howard Theater; she allowed me to go. Mary and I went together. The first live R&B show we saw was a performance by the Dells, whose big hit was "Oh What a Night." They opened for the Cadillacs. Their hit record was "Speedoo." Listening to the singers on the radio didn't do them justice. Seeing them in person brought them to life. The Howard Theater was the musical venue of our hearts. Finally, I could go inside.

In addition to Mama's permission to go to the Howard Theater, Mary and I had an unforgettable summer at Carrs Beach, Wilmer's Park, and Atlantic City, New Jersey, when my sophomore year ended. A bus left from Washington, D.C., and took us to Carrs Beach at least once during the summer. The cost of admission was ten cents and included concerts, swimming, and hayrides. Mary and I were only interested in the concerts. Most entertainers who performed close by came to Carrs Beach to perform once their gigs ended. We saw entertainers like Jackie Wilson, James Brown, Etta James, the Drifters, LaVern Baker, Fats Domino, Lloyd Price, the Cadillacs, and Chuck Berry from 1:00 p.m. until we boarded the bus at 5:00 p.m. to return home.

At Wilmer's Park in Brandywine, Maryland, one

entertainer we saw was the exceptional Sam Cooke, who had recently left his popular gospel group, the Soul Stirrers, to sing secular music. He sat under a tent between performances, and I had the opportunity to talk to him. I was amused that he was shy and uncomfortable in my presence. I guessed he was nervous because law enforcement targeted entertainers and locked them up if they disobeyed the Jailbait law. I was 15 and looked even younger. He became my favorite 1950s soul singer.

Mary and I also went to the boardwalk in Atlantic City, New Jersey, in the summer of 1958. That was before casinos came to New Jersey. Buses ran from designated spots in Washington, D.C., took people to Atlantic City, and returned them for a small fee. We walked on the boardwalk, and Mary talked to people she knew. I didn't see anyone I knew; moving had ruined my social life. I enjoyed being with Mary. As we walked on the boardwalk, we shopped at the vendors. We did not get in the water to ride the waves. The bus returned to Washington, D.C., at 5:00 p.m. sharp.

> *Up and down the boardwalk,*
> *Shopping and small talk:*
> *Riding the waves and bathing in the sun;*
> *Atlantic City, in the fifties, was fun.*

At the end of the summer of 1958 and the beginning of my junior year, I had fully developed into a woman.

The second week of school, I walked to the mom-and-pop neighborhood store at the end of the school day to buy a Coke and candy bar. I took a shortcut down a neighborhood street and passed by a boy tinkering under the hood of his car. As I passed by, he looked up and

Me and Spike

the smile on his handsome face was contagious, like a yawn. When he stood up, his slim, tall body mesmerized me. He said hello and asked my name. His name was William, but he called himself "Spike." He had dropped out of school and had a job. We chatted for a while, and when I was ready to go, he asked if he could visit me. I gave him my address. He did not have a telephone.

Spike visited me that night and almost every night thereafter. We became an item. Our first date was to the hot shop, where a waitress delivered orders to the car on roller skates. Their "Mighty Mo" sandwich was on the order of McDonald's Big Mac. Our second date was to a Little Tavern, known for its lip-licking ten-cent hamburgers about the size of a 50-cent piece. Spike visited me that night, and almost every night thereafter. We became an item. Our first date was to the Hot Shoppes, where a waitress delivered orders to the car on roller skates. Their "Mighty Mo" sandwich was on the order of McDonald's Big Mac. Our second date was to a Little Tavern, known for its lip-licking ten cent hamburgers about the size of a 50-cent piece.

On some weekends, Rita and her boyfriend, Bill, would go with Spike and me to a drive-in movie. At first, admission was a dollar for each car because the drive-in didn't provide car heaters. We brought blankets and cuddled to stay warm. Before long, the drive-in provided heaters, and the price of admission increased to a dollar per person. We giggled at patrons sneaking out of the trunks of cars to avoid paying the additional admission fee.

Also in my junior year, Aunt Clo and I began exercise competitions at her house. We climbed down a wall backward with our hands. We did headstands with our legs perfectly straight, jumping jacks, push-ups, and more. She was 21 years older than me, and I had gym every day, yet she usually did more repetitions. Once, after exercising, she measured the length of our big and second toes. Her second toe was longer than her big toe; mine were even. She said it meant she could hold on to her man longer than me. I was puzzled.

> *Auntie was my challenge in exercise,*
> *And she was wise:*
> *However, her second-toe theory*
> *I found it a bit fishy.*

I also turned 16 in October of my junior year, and since my birthday fell on a Saturday night, Almeta took me to my first nightclub. Being a minor, I could not consume alcohol, so I drank ginger ale. It was exciting to be in the nightclub with adults. Of course, Mama did not know Almeta had taken me to a nightclub. Mama, Spike, and I celebrated my birthday the next day.

During the winter school break of my junior year, Mary, Sudie, and I went to the Howard Theater to see James Brown. We stood in line in freezing temperatures; our feet were numb. James Brown's staff gave those in the queue a choice of coffee or hot chocolate. Once we were inside, we forgot about our numb feet. Mary was engaged to marry, but we went without boyfriends because we could scream and sing along. The Chantels opened for James Brown. They were the first girl group we had seen perform. Their big hit was "Maybe." Their gorgeous formal dresses sparkled. James Brown was immaculate in a white suit with glittering lapels, a cream shirt, a white tie, and cream shoes. "Please, Please, Please" was one song he performed. He sang and danced his behind off. Entertainers dressed to the nines in the 1950s. The entertainers of the 1950s, my fashionable flour sack dresses, and my Chinchilla coat Santa brought me at age six formed my style of dress.

> *Teenagers loved the Howard shows;*
> *The performance and the fine clothes:*
> *It was exciting and thrilling;*
> *The music expressed our feelings.*

At the end of my junior year, the summer of 1959, Rita, Bill, Spike, and I spent most nights at Hains Point. None of our homes had air conditioning, and nights during the summer were sweltering hot. Hains Point was a large park that divided Washington, D.C., and Virginia. It was also the home of the national cherry blossom festival and the city's Lover's Lane. On the Virginia side, we watched airplanes taxi for takeoff and land on the runway at Washington National Airport (renamed Reagan National in 1998). The airport lights were captivating. In the middle of the Virginia and DC sides of the park, there was an open grassy field. We bought sodas and snacks and slept there under the stars until daybreak. The end of the summer of 1959 was the last one I spent with Rita; I never saw her again. I don't know what happened to her. Bill became a champion roller skater at the historic Kalorama Road roller-skating rink.

The summer of 1959 was also when one of Great-Aunt Louise's sons visited and told me that Arthur Clay was not my father. He said, "Your daddy's name was

Arnett

Milton." He didn't provide a last name. Mama called him a bald-faced liar and told him that Arthur Clay was my daddy. She said, "You weren't there when I got pregnant." In addition to Great Aunt Dorothy's skepticism and Daddy's cruel beating at age six, my cousin planted further doubt in my mind. Yet, I wanted to believe Mama.

The summer of 1959, I met my cousin Arnett on T Street. He was the great-grandson of Great-Aunt Amanda, whom I had previously met in Baltimore, Maryland. His father, William Edward, known as "Bertie" (1931–1994), had started taking his son around to meet the family, just as Mama had done with me when I lived in Baltimore. We have kept in touch over the years.

Sudie and Mary also graduated from Tech in the summer of 1959, and Mary and her fiancé tied the knot in a no-frills private family ceremony. I was thrilled for Mary but sad that hanging out, as we had in the past, was over. My relationship with Sudie also changed; her mother became ill, and she became her caretaker.

Unfortunately, Butch passed away in the summer of 59, just before my senior year began. He came inside one day, laid down, and when Mama went to feed him, he was dead. He was only about two years old. We never knew whether he ate something poisonous outside or what happened. His tail was wagging, and he seemed fine before he went outside. May he rest in doggie Heaven.

On a cheerful note, Spike proposed and placed a flashy diamond ring on my finger at the beginning of my senior year. I said yes! I looked forward to a private June marriage following my graduation, similar to the private wedding Mary had. Neither my parents, Spike, nor I could afford a large wedding. I didn't want a big wedding. Being married to Spike, having a family, and settling down in one place was all I wanted, although I still planned to seek a job in the federal government.

> *My childhood was ending;*
> *And my adulthood was beginning.*
> *My dreams were coming true:*
> *Something borrowed, something blue.*

I had been engaged to Spike for about two weeks when Daddy announced we were moving to Harvard Street, NW, after living on T Street for over three years.

Me and Spike

I had friends, and I wanted to graduate in the summer from the same high school I had attended since tenth grade. Moving had started again, and I had begun my senior year. I had thought Daddy had no further need to punish me after Terry came to live with us. I was wrong. Why didn't Mama try to stop the madness? Something snapped inside of me! Without reason,

I quit Spike. Over the years, I realized that I quit him out of misdirected anger, and breaking up with him somehow eased the unbearable pain that resurfaced when I learned we were moving again. That breakup was probably my greatest regret in life. I have wondered what our lives would have been like had I graduated from Tech and we had married.

The move to Harvard Street, NW was my 14th move. Mama said I could catch the city bus to continue attending Tech. Spike learned where I moved and offered to drive me to and from school. I turned him down. The harder he tried to reunite us, the meaner I was to him. He eventually stopped coming around. I was in so much pain, I didn't care. I was glad to be attending Tech; I wanted badly to graduate from there. However, June was many months away.

A couple of weeks after moving to Harvard Street, I began forming a singing group, as music was a source of peace. I recruited Joyce. I asked her if she knew anyone else who would be interested; she didn't. Then, the second week, I boarded the bus to Tech, and the bus driver was the senior who drove the school bus at Richardson High School in Pendleton, Virginia. What were the odds? Four years had passed, but he remembered me. We engaged in small talk, and I asked him if he knew of a lead singer. He said he knew just the right person. I provided my phone number for him to give to the individual.

The following day, someone contacted me and auditioned over the phone. His name was Eugene "Gene." He was the right person. His voice was melodic and unique. Gene knew a bass singer and brought him to our first rehearsal the next day. The group ended up being superb natural first tenor and lead singer Gene, sweet soprano Joyce, me also a tenor, and an impressive baritone/bass that Gene brought to rehearsal. I have forgotten his name. I named the quartet The Crystals; we would sparkle around the world. We probably would have been the first mixed quartet of two girls and two guys. We rehearsed three nights a week on a ditty Gene had written entitled "Sylvia" to record. We also practiced the songs of recorded artists to build a repertoire. Our voices blended well.

The group was on a roll; then, on January 6, 1960, I heard my name over the public address system summoning me to report to the assistant principal's office. Daddy had withdrawn me from Tech five months away from graduation. I had already taken my photograph for the senior yearbook. I cried and begged Daddy; it fell on deaf ears.

My Yearbook Photo

The Crystals were disappointed that we were disbanding. We had worked hard on our songs for three months and were putting together a band and a promotional package to get jobs. Our dream of sparkling around the world was over! Nobody got the chance to hear us sing except Mama, and she had stayed out of sight in her room.

To add to my dilemma, Daddy was in the process of adopting Terry, and to our regret, Uncle Jesse Reed refused to grant permission. He did not want his son's surname to change. After we had him for almost four years, his father came to pick him up. We were heartbroken. Yet Mama did not try to stop Daddy from moving.

> *Daddy could not adopt Terry*
> *And my group I had to bury.*
> *Further, no graduation from Tech.*
> *What a shipwreck!*

My 15th move was back to Fort Belvoir for the third time. The public bus schedule made it impossible to catch the bus to Tech. I felt defeated and angry. I quit school. Mama cried and pleaded for me to complete high school. I knew how important it was to her. Mama had always been there for me, and I didn't want to disappoint her. I eventually gave in. I remembered Grampa's advice about picking my battles. I had grown older and understood what he meant. That was a battle I chose not to fight.

Once I decided to return to school, I called Mary to share what had happened. Other than letting her know we had moved, we had not talked for a few months. She was newly married, and I did not want to intrude. She said I would have been disappointed in myself later on had I dropped out of high school with just four months left to graduate. Mary told me she was expecting her first child in two months. I also talked to Sudie, who told me I needed a high school diploma to get a job in the federal government.

I enrolled in Luther Jackson High School in February 1960, the same school I had attended in the eighth grade. Jessie, my neighbor who had gone to Luther Jackson with me and taught me to smoke, had moved on. Pictures had already been taken for the yearbook, and if I wanted a school ring, I had to order it immediately. Mama talked to the principal and guidance counselor, who assigned research papers and projects for me to complete in addition to class work. I began the arduous task. As I finished the papers and projects, I submitted them for grading.

After I enrolled in Luther Jackson High School, Mama suggested I go to the Fort Belvoir Noncommissioned

Officer's Club (NCO) on the weekend to dance and have fun. I was allowed entrance as a 17-year-old as long as I did not consume alcohol. The follow-

Me

Jimmy

ing Sunday night, I walked to the NCO club alone. I sat at a table, and before long, a breathtaking soldier dressed in full uniform came to my table, stretched out his hand, and motioned his head toward the dance floor. I took his hand. At the end of the dance, he asked if he could join my table. He was Puerto Rican, and his name was Baldomero Jimenez. He called himself "Jimmy." We chatted, and at the end of the evening, he walked me to my door. He asked if he could visit me tomorrow, and we agreed on seven p.m. the next night. A fit man in a uniform was hard to resist. Jimmy was a bona fide soldier, unlike my first boyfriend. When we said goodnight, I was floating on a cloud.

> *I admired Jimmy at first glance*
> *And then he asked me to dance.*
> *Our meeting felt comfortable;*
> *Being together was inevitable.*

Jimmy knocked on the door at seven p.m. the next night and every weeknight afterward like clockwork. We were alone in the house. Daddy was working, and Mama was playing bingo. The curly black-haired dreamboat was nine years older than me. However, his and Grampa Reed's birthdays were on April 6, confirming that he was my destiny. Over the next several weeks, we talked, watched TV, and danced. As he worked on Saturdays, he often gave me money to go to Washington, D.C., to visit Aunt Clo and spend time with my friends. We went to the NCO club on Sunday nights. As we became closer, Jimmy assured me that his father taught him how to avoid getting a girl pregnant by using the withdrawal method. He said it worked, and a condom was not necessary.

The leader of the United Service Organization (USO) band, who was playing at the NCO club when  we met, was a friend of Jimmy's, and as I had told him I could sing, he arranged for me to sing a couple of songs with the band. There were no

Me

Sudie, Courtesy of Clarence Jones

rehearsals. I asked the band if they knew a song, and if not, I named another until it was one that they knew. One song I sang was a blues tune by Lloyd Price, "Lawdy Miss Clawdy." Two other songs were "Sweet Nothin's" by Brenda Lee and "Lucky Lips" by Ruth Brown. I had the blues when I met Jimmy. He kissed my lucky lips and whispered sweet nothings in my ear. After I sang for the first time, the band leader called me up to the bandstand every Sunday night thereafter to sing. One night, Sudie and a friend came to hear me sing. She was surprised. Of the T Street girls, only Joyce had heard me sing; Mary, Sudie, and Almeta had not.

At the end of two months, the USO band leader asked if I was interested in traveling with them and singing with the band. I responded yes. Given that I was a minor, he handed me a permission form for Mama to sign. Mama said I promised to finish high school. She refused to sign it. The band completed their contract at the NCO club and moved on to their next gig without me. In hindsight, Mama's refusal to let me join the band was perhaps a blessing. I was naive, with little street knowledge and no knowledge of the music business. On the flip side, I had no say.

Wanted by Sister Rosetta Tharpe;
The Crystals and we were sharp;
Roy Hamilton and the USO Band;
Still, my singing career was canned.

As I worked to complete high school, my parents had made plans to go to Germany via Saint Louis, Missouri. Because Mama didn't want me to quit school again, I didn't learn about it until it was time to apply for passports. Daddy wanted us to live in Saint Louis where his sister, Lucille, lived, while he went to Germany and waited for living quarters. He asked her to find an apartment for us.

Once I learned about Germany, I told my Home Economics teacher I was going abroad, and she planned a Bon Voyage celebration. The class took me to *The Ten Commandments*, starring Charlton Heston and Yul Brynner, at the historical Warner Theater in Washington, D.C. Seeing the movie with my classmates was a fantastic send-off. The event commemorated my few months at Luther Jackson High. I never saw any of them again.

Following the sendoff, Mama took our birth certificates out of safekeeping, and we applied for passports. Mama shared two certificates of my birth with me. One listed my name as Rachel Louise Cooper and the other as Rachel Louise Clay. My name was Louise; why was the first name Rachel on both of my birth certificates? I was confused. I was also confused about my last name. Mama explained:

> You already knew everyone called you Louise because you were born in Aunt Louise's house. What you didn't know was that I named you Rachel Louise. Rachel was your great-great grandmother's name. I enrolled you in schools as Louise Rachel until the seventh grade, after which I enrolled you as Rachel Louise and asked school officials to call you Louise. I gave you my last name, Cooper, at birth because your daddy and I were not married until you were six. After we married, Arthur and I went to the Office of Vital Records in Richmond, Virginia, the summer before you started

first grade in 1949, and he swore under
oath that he was your birth father. The
court changed your name from Cooper to
Clay and sealed your original birth record,
requiring a court order to open it.

I contemplated Daddy's declaration, made under
oath, that he was my biological father. In that manner,
he became my legal dad, and he would not have to
adopt me for me to become his dependent. I still did not
believe he was my biological father. I was disillusioned
at six, and nothing had changed. I was 17 and didn't
feel loved by my dad. However, I kept my thoughts to
myself.

Next, I saw Mama and Daddy's birth certificates,
which revealed their ages. Mama was 18 years younger. I
knew Daddy was older because he remained 39 through-
out my primary and secondary school years; the age he
and his favorite comedian, Jack Benny, decided to stay
forever. However, I would not have guessed he was
that many years older than Mama. She said, "A young
woman is an old man's darling."

> *Information on my birth certificate*
> *Revealed something significant:*
> *My first name was not the same;*
> *I had only known my middle name.*

After we finished our passport applications, Mama probed about my last menstrual cycle. Her suspicion was correct; Jimmy's withdrawal birth control method had failed. I knew now what Mama meant by "Keep your pocketbook shut." I also know what one consequence was for opening it. Mama decided not to tell Daddy right away. I welcomed her decision. It gave me time to tell Jimmy. By the time Mama informed Daddy, I hoped we would be married.

When I told Jimmy we were having a baby, he told me he was married with three children. He had not told me earlier because they had been separated for some time and his family had returned to Puerto Rico. All I knew was I loved Jimmy and wanted my baby. He said he loved me too, and he would file for divorce and marry me as soon as it was final. I felt outraged that he had not told me he was married, disappointed, surprised, worried, and in a pickle, but as we loved each other, I was hopeful that we would soon be married.

The next day, I informed Mama Jimmy was married but that he was getting a divorce and intended to marry me. However, I feared Daddy would put me out when he learned I was pregnant. Mama told me not to worry; she would talk to Daddy. She encouraged me to hold my head up. She said, "One pregnancy out of wedlock is a mistake; two is a habit." Mama continued, "The baby might not have a daddy, but it will have two mothers."

The discovery of my pregnancy and the completion of high school came simultaneously. I bid my instructors and fellow students farewell and gave Aunt Clo's address to the principal's office to mail my diploma. Mama was satisfied that I finished high school, and I hoped Jimmy would marry me before I left Saint Louis for Germany.

> *I was not a part of the prom celebration,*
> *Or the high school graduation:*
> *My picture wasn't even in the yearbook;*
> *A ring and a diploma were what I took.*

TEN

LIVED ABROAD

The train arrived in Saint Louis, and a taxicab took us to Aunt Lucille's house. Daddy introduced her to Mama and me, and she prepared lunch for us. She called her brother Buddy. I noticed her tall frame and flawless white teeth. We finished eating, and Auntie drove us to the two-bedroom apartment on Page Boulevard she had rented for Mama and me, complete with a pink Princess telephone in the living room. That place was my 16th abode. We put our luggage inside, and Aunt Lucille drove us to the grocery store just up the street. It was within walking distance. I could not believe I was pregnant and living in Saint Louis.

Daddy left Saint Louis for Germany the next week, and Auntie promised to look out for us. His older sister took charge. Aunt Lucille drove us around Saint Louis and across the Mississippi River bridge to East Saint Louis, another city in Illinois. At the end of our tour, Mama asked Auntie to show us how to catch bus transportation to the military hospital. I needed to begin prenatal care. I was nearing my third month of pregnancy.

Mama and I settled into our new living quarters in Saint Louis, and I wrote to Mary, giving her my address in Saint Louis, updating her on my situation, and asking if she had a boy or a girl. Her baby should have been about two months old. I disclosed my pregnancy to Mary and told her I felt happy. On the other hand, I was ashamed that I was pregnant out of wedlock. I didn't keep in touch with Sudie, Almeta, or Joyce, and I asked Mary not to tell them about my pregnancy. The fewer people who knew, the less likely Spike would find out. I did not want him to know.

I also wrote to Jimmy to give him my new address, and we communicated often. He put a little cash in each of his letters. Jimmy stated that he had no preference for a name or sex. Since I wanted a girl, I began to refer to the baby as "Toni." I had decided on Tonya if I had a girl and Tony if I had a boy. He seemed as excited as I was about our pregnancy. Mama sent Jimmy's letters to the Pentagon inquiring about child support. We sent the originals as there was no way to make copies. No Xerox machines existed for public use.

In July, Jimmy wrote and sent money for me to travel to Washington, D.C., on the train. He wanted to talk to me. I told Mama, and she decided to go with me to visit her sister, Clo, one last time. I responded to

Jimmy's letter and told him what day I would be there. I wondered what he wanted to talk about. I was sure that it was in my best interest. I couldn't wait to get to Washington, D.C.

> *Jimmy must have filed for divorce,*
> *And was waiting for it to be in force.*
> *What else could it be about?*
> *Our time was running out.*

We arrived at Aunt Clo's, and I called Jimmy. He came to pick me up. When he knocked on the door, Mama asked if she could talk to him; I was not invited. They went into another room. Jimmy came out looking defeated; he told me Mama blamed him for my pregnancy. He said she told him he was nine years older than me and should've known to use a condom. She also cursed him for being a married man. She let Jimmy know, in no uncertain terms, that Toni and I were her responsibility. He grumbled, "You mudder (sic) talk mean to me." Jimmy left. I did not get the chance to hear what he wanted to talk to me about. Mama nullified my reason for coming to Washington, D.C.

Mama waited until Jimmy left before she came out of the room. She had a look of satisfaction on her face. She had decided what was best for my baby and me without my input. I wasn't the kind of child who sassed

Mama. To go against her would have been disrespect-
ful. She was doing what she thought was best for us.

Aunt Clo had received my diploma from Luther
Jackson and gave it to me after Jimmy left. It symbol-
ized my perseverance through 14 primary and second-
ary schools excluding kindergarten in Evington. I was
grateful to Luther Jackson High School for allowing me
to earn a high school diploma. Nevertheless, I attended
Tech as a sophomore, junior, and half of my senior year,
compared to about three months at Luther Jackson; and
my picture was in Tech's yearbook. I was a Techite.

Before leaving DC, I visited Mary and showed her
my diploma. I also expressed my feelings regarding
Jimmy. I told her that perhaps Jimmy had filed for his di-
vorce, and if Mama had not gotten involved, we might
have been a family and raised our baby together. Mary
told me it would work out in the end. She said every-
thing happened the way it was supposed to. Her son
was two months old. I asked her how it felt to be a
mother. She loved it and was happy. She was glad that
he was finally sleeping through the night. Mary wished
me a safe trip on the train back to Saint Louis and prom-
ised to stay in contact.

The train ride back to Saint Louis was dishearten-
ing. I pretended to be asleep to avoid talking to Mama.
Part of me felt going with Mama was the best option for
Toni and me. The other part wished Mama had given

Jimmy and me a chance to work our situation out. I loved Jimmy; he was my destiny. Riding home on the train felt like Cupid was dragging my heart over miles of poisonous train tracks.

Daddy telephoned from Germany the night we returned to Saint Louis. Mama disclosed I was pregnant, and I heard him respond, "We'll do the best we can." Mama did not ask for his assistance; he volunteered. A man who'd shown me little kindness and who, in my mind, did not like me had offered to provide for me and Toni. I was humbled. He did not tell Mama that I had to make it on my own.

> *Following the telephone call,*
> *Daddy wasn't a monster, after all:*
> *He didn't put me out;*
> *It was a humbling turnabout.*

Daddy came around, but Jimmy did not answer my calls or respond to my letters. Mama did what she thought was best for me, and I did not want her to think I didn't appreciate it. I cried at night alone in my room. I wanted to be with Jimmy, and he had washed his hands of Toni and me. I was helpless and in misery. There was nothing I could do.

Three months after we returned to St. Louis from DC, I turned 18. Mama bought cake and ice cream. On the cake, she put two candles, one for me and one for Toni. Aunt Lucille came and joined Mama in singing Happy Birthday. After Aunt Lucille left, I confessed to Mama that I started smoking at age 13; Mama frowned, rolled her eyes toward the ceiling, and stated, "I suspected back then that my cigarettes were disappearing." We laughed! She wanted to know if I still smoked. I assured her I had quit when I learned I was pregnant. I knew it was not healthy for my baby.

The day after my birthday, Aunt Lucille informed Mama that I would have to fly to Germany posthaste because after I was seven months pregnant, I would have to wait until after the baby was born. Mama did not want to stay in Saint Louis any longer, and when Daddy called the next day, she asked him to prepare for us to travel immediately. In a couple of days, he called and said he had made the arrangements and had found somewhere for us to live until military quarters were ready. We thanked Aunt Lucille for her help and she took us to the airport.

The airplane we boarded was an old, gray military aircraft that shook and rattled like a car with a flat tire. It was the first airplane ride for both of us. Mama and I tried to be strong by putting on our bravest faces for each other. We stopped in Newfoundland to refuel, and the pilot evacuated the plane. Mama and I purchased a soda and a snack, and in about ten minutes, the flight was reboarding. We were concerned about the quick turnaround.

> *A ten-minute repair;*
> *And we were back in the air?*
> *How could it be repaired?*
> *We were scared.*

Like in the 1942 movie *The Flying Tigers* we landed in Frankfurt on a wing and a prayer; ambulances and fire engines aligned the airport in readiness. We were relieved to get off the dilapidated military aircraft. Thank God, we landed safely. It was a heart-pounding experience. Neither Mama nor I ever wanted to board another military plane.

Daddy picked us up and drove us to a northern city called Kassel. There were no speed limits on the autobahn barring postings for lower speeds for safety precautions. Daddy didn't drive faster than 55 miles per hour, no matter what. On the way, I saw exquisite architectural designs and beautifully landscaped farmland. The terrain was flat, smooth, and sectioned off. However, I missed T Street.

Daddy was stationed at Rothwesten Air Base; a clandestine place. Adolf Hitler had selected the area in 1935 to construct Germany's first flying school and fighter strip. The United States Infantry Troops that air base in 1945, and were the first American unit to operate aircraft on German soil. [6] Daddy told us that the military still found Hitler's hidden mines from time to time and dismantled them.

As military quarters were still unavailable, Daddy rented two rooms on the second floor of a house in Kassell, Germany, about five miles from where he worked. The owner lived on the ground floor and grew hogs in the cellar. The stench was worse than human feces. Daddy said that was all he could find close to where he worked. It helped a little bit to keep my hand cupped over my nose and mouth, as much as possible. I hoped Toni did not detect the scent inside of me. It was my 17th residence.

> *We lived above a pigsty.*
> *Stench! My, oh my!*
> *Daddy had put us in foul play.*
> *He said there was no other way.*

In two weeks, the military rescued us from the pig-pens; they relocated Daddy to a military base in Kornwestheim, Germany, and moved us to temporary living quarters nearby in Ludwigsburg, Germany. It had eight bedrooms to accommodate a large or small family. I embraced my 18th move. It was about four hours away from the pigsty. We were careful not to

---

[6] Rothwesten Air Base, Germany and 601st AC & W Squadron, History, http://www.601st-615th-acw.org/history.htm (accessed April 26, 2016).

occupy but two bedrooms to reduce the thorough cleaning required to pass the military inspection when we received permanent quarters. Daddy believed military quarters would be available soon after Toni's birth.

Mama took me to a military doctor for a check-up once we moved into our temporary quarters. He  wanted to send me approximately two hours away to a hotel near the 97th General Military Hospital in Frankfurt, Germany the day after Christmas. To be an American citizen, the baby had to be born in a military hospital. Otherwise, I would not have been able to take her to America. Toni's due date was not until January 25th, so I begged to wait until January 2nd. I was in a foreign country, and I wanted to be with my family on the New Year. The doctor reluctantly agreed.

Me at 8 months

I wrote to Mary and shared the unbelievable pigpen story. I also wrote to Jimmy, hoping he would respond since he knew our baby's birth was nearing. I wondered how different my life might've been had Mama allowed Jimmy to work out his marital situation. I wished we could have raised our baby together.

On Christmas Eve, Daddy took Mama and me to purchase a Christmas tree and decorations. We were successful along with the use of our English-to-German translation book and body language. The merchant helped Daddy tie the large tree to the top of the car, and a neighbor helped him take it inside. Mama and I decorated it, and Daddy topped it with a blinking Star of David. For the first time, the three of us enjoyed Christmas together. In previous years, it had been Mama and me. Daddy had either been at work or he didn't participate.

> *My life had changed drastically;*
> *Daddy and I were living in harmony,*
> *And I was in Germany,*
> *A mother shortly to be.*

The week after Christmas, Daddy took Mama and me shopping again for baby items. Toni was about three weeks away from making her entrance. We found a reversible crib/playpen and a large crib mobile with colorful toy balls. We also found infant clothing and everything else my baby would need. I was ready to go to Frankfurt the following week to bring my baby home.

As January 2nd was on a Monday and the military van from Ludwigsburg to Frankfurt ran on Tuesdays and Thursdays, Mama and I decided to wait two more days. I left on Thursday, January 5, 1961. Mama rode with me. It was 87 kilometers to the Hotel Ambassador Arms in Frankfurt, Germany, across from the military hospital where my baby would be born. Military dependents with medical concerns only had to pay $1.00 a day out of pocket.

Mama visited on Tuesday and delivered a letter from Mary telling me that Spike had gotten married. I wished him the best. I ended our engagement for no reason and broke his heart. Mary had also given birth to a baby girl. Her son and daughter were ten months apart. On Thursday, January 20, 1961, Mama brought a letter from Jimmy. It read, "You might as well forget about me; I'm married now." Forget! How? I was waiting to deliver our child any day. I tore the note into pieces and flushed it down the toilet, but the words were branded in my brain. I did wonder, however, how he could have divorced and remarried in six months.

In two days, our daughter was born on Sunday, January 22, 1961, at 3:44 a.m. at the 97th General Hospital in Frankfurt, Germany. The nurse handed me a 4x3-inch pink card advertising Pet Milk that listed Tonya's weight as six-pounds and four ounces, and her length as 19 and 3/4 inches long. It also recorded the outside temperature at 32.2 degrees Fahrenheit. I named her Tonya Everene Clay. Tonya was a slight variation of Sonya the name of the last doll baby I received for Christmas in 1953 in West Virginia. I gave her Mama's middle name. Looking into my baby girl's face, I saw her gorgeous father reaching for my hand motioning me to the dance floor at the NCO club at Fort Belvoir when we met. It felt like long ago.

> *Pretty as a daisy;*
> *A real live doll baby.*
> *A bundle of love;*
> *Sent from above.*

I was at the 97th General Hospital for two weeks; my hospital stay ended on February 7, 1961. I had attended classes on how to care for my baby: feeding, burping, diaper changing, and much more. Mama picked me up in the military van. Snow flurries were falling lightly at first and escalated to a storm. The van slipped and slid most of the way home. It was a rough ride, but we arrived home in one piece. Tonya slept through it all. Daddy peeped at her, shook his shoulders, and chuckled; he was afraid to hold a newborn.

Once home, I wrote to Jimmy and Mary to announce Tonya's birth and congratulate her on her second baby. Mary responded with joy for me; Jimmy did not respond. I felt empty inside. Mama encouraged me not to let one mistake hold me back. She wanted me to go on with my life. I didn't see my daughter as a mistake; I saw her as my life. I didn't feel as lonely anymore. However, that was another battle I chose not to fight. I believed Mama meant well; she was trying to spare me from what she went through.

To please Mama, I walked around the neighbor-hood. I was impressed by the cleanliness of the German people. They hung their bed linens out the window for airing and swept the sidewalks and areas surrounding their homes daily. I met a 16-year-old German boy named Chris, who was also walking. He spoke fluent English and was an accomplished musician. He enlightened me that a German student who did not wish to attend the Universität had to choose a vocation; he chose music. We became buddies. He visited, met my parents, rocked Tonya, and taught me German words and phrases.

Chris

About two months after meeting Chris, the military notified Daddy that we had permanent living quarters in Stuttgart, Germany, less than ten miles from where we lived in Ludwigsburg. Chris and I did not stay in touch. I have wondered whether he became a famous musician. He was a swell person.

Our Stuttgart apartment had three bedrooms. Tonya and I had separate rooms. After living with pigs and in temporary quarters with eight bedrooms, my 19th move was welcomed. Although I still missed T Street, I felt better about being in Germany. Daddy invited me to accompany him to Robinson Barracks, where he worked. He had some business to take care of regarding the move. It was a few miles from our living quarters. I was surprised at how Tonya's birth had turned our relationship around. Daddy had never asked me to go anywhere with him before. Mama kept Tonya.

We entered Robinson Barracks, and a striking, brawny soldier greeted us and introduced himself as Paul. Daddy went to take care of his business, and Paul told him he would take care of me. I told Paul my name, and we chatted. Daddy returned shortly, and Paul gave me his contact information as we were leaving. I was hesitant about meeting another soldier.

I called Paul after we received and unpacked our household goods. That uniform! He told me he lived in the barracks and was single. He was amusing, complementary, and also a music lover. He was from Detroit, Michigan, and his family sent him the latest Motown records. I missed the onset of Motown music while working to complete high school and then preparing to go abroad. After a short while, I gave him my address.

Paul visited and introduced me to the Motown sound. I had brought my Fifties records and record player. I loved Motown music as much as Fifties music. Of the Motown singers that Paul played, my favorite was the Miracles, whose lead singer was Smokey Robinson. Their latest record was "Shop Around." When the record finished playing, Paul said he was through shopping around; he had found his girl.

Several months passed, and Paul impressed me and my parents. On my 19th birthday, Mama and Paul gave

Tonya's first steps

me a birthday party. Tonya took her first steps that night. She was only nine months old. Me and Mama were surprised! Daddy shook his shoulders and chuckled. She held onto my finger to steady herself and walked until she eventually tuckered herself out. Once she fell asleep, my neighbors and I partied

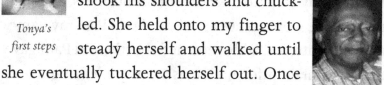

Daddy

well into the night. There was plenty of food, ice cream, cake, and alcohol. Paul brought the music. The party was on!

> *Although I was hesitant,*
> *Paul offered merriment:*
> *He won my heart*
> *In Stuttgart.*

The day following my 19th birthday, Mama announced she was four months pregnant. Mama had begun to wear baggy clothes; I thought it was her new style. After I was grown, and she had not had another baby, there was no reason to suspect she was pregnant. My eyes popped. Mama was 36, and Daddy was fifty-four. Their granddaughter was nine months old. I was baffled. However, I congratulated Mama. She explained that she and Daddy learned of fertility treatments that the military hospital provided in Germany that were not available in America. That was why Daddy requested a tour of duty in Germany. Further, because of Mama's heart condition, doctors in America would not have helped her to conceive.

After the explanation, I understood why we moved to Fort Belvoir. The military would not have packed our household goods to travel abroad unless we lived on a military base. It remained a mystery why we moved from T Street to Harvard Street between waiting to move to Fort Belvoir. I also still didn't understand why my parents didn't wait another few months so that I could have graduated from Tech.

When Mama learned she was pregnant, she did not tell the doctor who had helped her and Daddy. She feared something would go wrong, and they would abort the fetus. She said she carried me to term and could do it again. Mama sought prenatal care when she was five months pregnant. Her doctor hospitalized her for the duration of her pregnancy. She was determined to have her baby.

★ ★ ★

Paul got military leave for New Year's Day and took me out on the town to a New Year's Eve celebration at the Bahnhof. Daddy babysat Tonya. There was a marching band on the first floor of the train station and a dance band on the second. Paul and I went to the second floor. Paul spoke some German, and I understood a bit more. The people were friendly, and we all partied together. Paul was in uniform, and the German people respected the American uniform. At 20 minutes to midnight, celebrants on the ground floors commenced marching up and down the steps. Those on the second floor joined in. The marching continued until the clock struck midnight. Then, everyone held hands and watched the spectacular fireworks display outside as the band played Auld Lang Syne. When the fireworks ended, Paul and I left. It was the only time Paul had taken me out on the town. It was memorable to join the German people in Stuttgart as they celebrated New Year's Eve.

> *Dancing, singing, and marching,*
> *And the band was swinging.*
> *What a beautiful lasting memory*
> *Of me and my soldier boy in Germany.*

In February of the New Year, I read in the Stars and Stripes military newspaper that John Glenn was the first American to orbit Earth. I was proud and excited about America's accomplishment. The next month I learned that Great-Aunt Dorothy, who kept me in Baltimore in the 1940s, had been killed in an automobile accident. She and Uncle Shep had gone to a funeral in North Carolina. They were on the way home when the accident occurred on Route 1, not far from Bowling Green, Virginia, where we lived in 1955. She was 55; Uncle Shep survived.

In the same month as Great-Aunt Dorothy's tragic accident, my only sibling entered the world on Sunday, March 25, 1962, almost 20 years younger than me. She weighed only four pounds but was healthy. Mama named her Wanda Cloteal. Wanda was the name of the nurse who cared for her during her four months of hospitalization, and Cloteal, of course, was her sister's name. Wanda's thick, curly, black hair nearly covered her forehead. After two weeks of observation, the doctor discharged her to Daddy. Mama remained in the hospital.

As Daddy was afraid to hold tiny babies, I brought Wanda home from the hospital. He just looked at her, shook his shoulders, and smiled, as he had when I brought Tonya home. Wanda could not get enough to eat; she drained her bottle and cried for more between feedings. I called Mama the next day, and she told me to go to the commissary and get some Pablum Baby Cereal to add to her milk formula; that satisfied her.

The following week, the doctor medevacked Mama to Walter Reed in Washington, D.C., without her baby. Mama's delivery had been successful, but because of

Mama's heart condition, her doctor was not taking a chance on Mama having a setback. I was surprised! I thought Mama's doctor would observe her for a couple of weeks, discharge her, and we would serve out Daddy's three-year tour of duty. We had a little more than a year to go. Instead, Daddy had to arrange for us to return home as soon as possible. Paul helped with the babies and the housing inspection.

I wrote to Mary to notify her of Wanda's birth and that we were coming home shortly. I also shared that I didn't know how I would find the strength to leave Paul behind. She wrote back and said I had to do what I had to do and that God would give me the strength. Mary informed me that Sudie and Joyce had moved; she didn't know where. She said they had moved almost a year ago.

Within two weeks, Daddy had completed the arrangements for us to return home. My last night in

Germany was a nightmare. At age 19, I was leaving a man I loved for the third time because we were moving. Paul wiped my eyes, and I dabbed his. He only had a few months left in Germany to complete his tour of duty. He vowed he would come where I was as soon as he got home, and we would be married. I gave him Aunt Clo's telephone number where he could reach me. As Shakespeare

Me about 1962

wrote in Romeo and Juliet, parting was such sweet sorrow. Paul had to leave to get back to the base; I cried all night.

> Paul said we would marry,
> Making leaving easier to carry.
> However, our last night,
> Was a sad, gloomy sight.

ELEVEN

RETURNED TO AMERICA
WORK AND FIRST HUSBAND

Daddy, Tonya, Wanda, and I arrived at Aunt Clo's on T Street in Washington, D.C., on June 30, 1962. We had left for Germany a family of three, although I was still pregnant, but returned a family of five. Unlike my first airplane ride on the rickety military plane, my second airplane ride was smooth, pleasant, and without incident. Daddy had arranged with Aunt Clo for us to live with her until military quarters were ready at Fort Belvoir. He dropped us off and went directly to get Mama discharged from Walter Reed. Auntie oohed and aahed as she met her namesake and great-niece. Auntie's twins were 13, and Kaye was eight. We were all glad to see one another. Daddy had nicknamed Wanda Ninny Baby, so when Mama arrived at Auntie's, she nicknamed her Nee-Nee. Everybody called Wanda Nee-Nee henceforth, except Daddy, who continued to call her by his pet name.

T Street was different. The United States Armed Forces had deployed many young men in the neighborhood to the Vietnam War, and Sudie and Joyce had moved. I saw Grace, a friend of Sudie's, who had moved to T Street. I asked her about Sudie and Joyce's whereabouts. She didn't know where Sudie went and had never met Joyce. Grace met Tonya, Nee-Nee, and the rest of my family. She and I stayed in contact intermittently over the years. After chatting with Grace, it was time to take Tonya to meet my Huckleberrya friend, Almeta, and Mary's two children.

Grace, Courtesy of Grace Peters

Shortly after Tonya and I returned to Aunt Clo's from Mary's, Paul called from Germany to inquire if we had arrived safely. We were like love-sick puppies, although we couldn't talk long because of the expense. He called two additional times and then apparently reality set in that we were living in different countries. I wrote several letters but did not hear from Paul again. We had been inseparable for over a year in Germany, and he did an about-face in less than a month. Paul was the second soldier to dupe me. I was crushed.

> *I gave up on a military man,*
> *I needed a better plan:*
> *Two soldiers and an impersonator,*
> *Each one had been a rainmaker.*

About a week later, Mary, Almeta, and I walked to the Howard Theater to see the Temptations and others perform. It was wonderful being back at the Howard Theater! I had heard the Temptations sing on the records Paul played in Germany from his Motown collection. They sang "Ol' Man River" and the harmony was unforgettable. They wore white gloves, and the spotlight was on their gloves as they sang and acted out the song. Although Smokey Robinson and the Miracles were my favorite Motown group, after seeing the Temptations perform, there was a slim margin between my first and second choices.

Later that summer, Smokey Robinson and the Miracles performed at the Howard, and Mary went with me to see them. Smokey had become my favorite singer in Germany when I heard him sing "Shop Around." Paul told me that he had stopped shopping around when he met me. The Miracles were four guys and a girl. I remember they wore blue cord suits; the female wore a matching skirt. There were other singers on the show, but I don't recall who they were.

Daddy received notice at the end of August that housing would be available at Fort Belvoir in September. We were more than ready to be in our own home. Although I had enjoyed being back on T Street since we returned from Germany, my life had changed; T

Street was my past. I needed to find a job to take care of my daughter.

The move to Fort Belvoir was my 20th address. I was curious about what had changed my fourth time living at Fort Belvoir, so I took Tonya for a walk; she was 20 months old. To my astonishment, I saw Jimmy standing inside the glass doors of the NCO Club. He spied me, exited the doors, and ran. I stood there, startled! He must have been stunned to see me, as Daddy's tour of duty in Germany was for three years, and we returned in two. I headed home in disgust at the way Jimmy acted. I looked back, and he was stretching his neck to see Tonya. I made a U-turn so he could see his daughter, and he sprinted again as if a poisonous snake was chasing him.

> *My chance sighting of Jimmy was wild;*
> *How could he not want to see his child?*
> *He had turned coldhearted*
> *Since we parted.*

I told Mama what happened. It angered her, and she took Jimmy to court for child support. Jimmy and his wife had a lawyer, and we didn't. Jimmy denied Tonya; the judge cited the bastardy law and dismissed the case. Bam! The gavel slammed! The day in court was a waste of time. It was as if I had committed a crime.

After court, I began to look for a job. Daddy told us he was retiring and moving to Washington, D.C., within the next six months. I needed to earn enough money to attend a business school to refresh my typing and shorthand skills. I had been out of school for two years and needed to increase my chances of finding federal employment as a secretary when we relocated to D.C. A colonel hired me to do domestic work for him and his wife. I worked five days a week; they paid me $8.00 a day plus car fare. They had three children, and if they had a party on the weekend, I received extra if I babysat. They entertained often.

When Daddy retired in March of 1963, I had worked for three months. Our 21st move was to 10th and R Streets, NW, Washington, D.C. I enrolled in the Cortez Peters Outstanding Typist and shorthand courses with the

Tonya's 4th Birthday Party

money I earned doing domestic work. Daddy enjoyed retirement for three months and returned to the workforce. Mama cared for Tonya and Nee-Nee

Cousin Gladys

while Daddy worked, and I attended business college. When Tonya turned four, we had a family get-together, and cousin Gladys (1912–1988) came. Nee-Nee was almost three, and as seen in the picture, she had her eyes on that cake.

Within Three months, I completed Cortez Peters

with a typing speed of 90 words per minute on a Remington Rand manual typewriter. However, my shorthand speed was only 45 words per minute; it was passing, but the speed was low. I scored high on the federal entrance examination and the typing test, which enabled me to apply for clerk-typist jobs. I had to increase my shorthand speed before applying for a secretarial job.

After submitting several job applications, I learned Mary had also applied for federal employment. While waiting for a job interview, we decided to commemo-

Mary

rate our T Street years with one last round of fun. We boarded a steamboat off the pier of Main Street in SW Washington, D.C., to Marshall Hall. In addition to an amusement park, Marshall Hall was one of the few places excluding Nevada that had legal slot machines in the United States except for Nevada. Marshall Hall had hundreds of slot machines, including the penny machines that Mary and I played. The hour-and-a-half trip each way gave us plenty of time to reminisce. There was also entertainment, dancing, and music on board the steamboat.

> *Our tribute was enjoyable,*
> *But it was undeniable:*
> *That our teenage years were over,*
> *It was time for a makeover.*

I got an interview, and the U.S. Department of Agriculture (USDA) hired me in July 1963. It was a temporary summer job, but I had my foot in the door. As I used my first name on the job application, employees called me by my first name, Rachel. It took me a while to get used to my first name because I had been called by my middle name all my life. I told Mary about my name change, and she also began calling me Rachel. She thought Rachel sounded more sophisticated than Louise. Gratefully, we had both found jobs.

The boss' secretary supervised me. When she didn't have work for me, she loaned me out to other agencies. I arrived at work early every morning and got coffee for my boss, the secretary, and myself before the secretary assigned me to a work area. One morning, I ran in the door with seconds to spare, and the secretary was on her way down to get coffee for the boss. I asked her to bring me a cup, and she ignored me. From that day forward, I stopped getting coffee for them. I thought I was being nice; I didn't know it was one of my job responsibilities. being nice; I didn't know it was one of my job responsibilities.

After I had been on the job for a month, I wanted to attend Dr. Martin Luther King, Jr.'s March on Washington at the Lincoln Memorial and asked for the day off. My boss turned the request down; I went anyway. The march was exhilarating, and the magnitude of the audience was overwhelming. My boss did not reprimand me for walking off the job, at least not immediately.

After the March on Washington, I began applying to federal agencies again for a permanent job because my summer job was ending soon. Having scored high on the federal entrance examination and with three months of experience, I did not get an interview. What was I doing wrong? In the interim, a coworker told me about a job opportunity in the private sector. A small business owner of a wig store in Washington, D.C., hired me to manage the store, sell the wigs, and do the accounting. He provided training, and despite my poor math abilities, I grasped how to keep the books and enjoyed managing the wig store. It was a learning experience, and I earned a salary, although it was not the federal government job I desired.

Shortly after I started working at the wig store, an assassin murdered President John F. Kennedy in Dallas, Texas, on November 22, 1963. I was stunned and saddened. The sight of John-John, his three-year-old son, saluting his father's caisson was a lasting memory. Along with the rest of the world, I was in shock.

After working at the wig store for about a month, I learned of a job at US News and World Report. I applied and received an interview. The interviewer knew I had not been able to get a job. He could not tell me what my

boss at USDA said about me, only that it was an unde-
sirable supervisory appraisal. I told him there were two
possibilities why, and neither had anything to do with
job performance:

> *I refused to fetch the boss coffee*
> *And walked off the job to march in the rally:*
> *As such, my job applications were blocked*
> *Causing employment doors to be locked.*

When I finished my story, the interviewer asked if
I knew another supervisor at USDA that I could list on
my application. The boss' secretary loaned me to other
USDA offices, so I listed another supervisor on future
applications. Thanks to the kind interviewer, I soon
got a permanent job in the federal government. The
Department of Public Welfare (DPW) called me for an
interview and hired me.

I started working at DPW off Georgia Avenue, NW,
in January 1964 as a Dictaphone Machine Transcriber.
Social workers went to the homes of welfare recipients
and dictated their observations into a Dictaphone ma-
chine. I was one of several transcribers hired to tran-
scribe their dictations.

Not long after I was employed, I stopped in a neigh-
borhood tavern one Friday evening for Happy Hour
before heading home for the weekend. Sitting at the bar
was a guy talking non-stop about Cassius Clay winning

the World Heavyweight Boxing Championship three days ago. (He became Muhammad Ali the next month.) I sat at the bar, ordered a glass of wine, and we toasted the champ. I told him my last name was Clay, and he bought the next round. He was curious about whether I was related to the champ. He told me his name was Charles, and we moved to a booth and chit-chatted. I strung him along for a while before I told him I knew of no kinship to the champ. The charming, handsome, almond-eyed man and I exchanged telephone numbers before I dashed off.

Charles

Charles called the next day and asked if he could visit. I invited the charmer over. We found common ground. He was also familiar with T Street, where I had lived in the 1950s. He made me laugh. He was an Air Force veteran, but at least he wasn't wearing a military uniform. Charles began to visit often; we became friends and eventually an item. He took me to the Howard, other venues, and dancing. We fell in love.

The following year, on the last Saturday in January of 1965, Mama and I carried Tonya and Nee-Nee to Chattaroy to meet Grampa Reed. Tonya had just had her fourth birthday, and Nee was almost three. Tonya was his first great-granddaughter. Grampa was seriously ill from years of mining coal. He perked up when he saw the girls. Grampa had married a third wife, whom he introduced as "Coots." I never knew another name. I returned home the following day because I didn't have any leave. I had to report to work on Monday. Mama stayed to help Coots.

Grampa John Reed Cooper, Sr. took a turn for the worse and succumbed to silicotuberculosis on March 10, 1965, according to his death record. Working in the coal mine had taken its toll. I remembered Grampa Reed as strong, healthy, and full of life the way I knew him in Chattaroy in the summer of 1953 and Pendleton in the fall of 1955. I saw all my aunts and uncles at the funeral except Uncle Charles. Gramma Anniebell and Aunt Hazel did not attend. I stored Grampa Reed in the first chamber of my heart so that he would always be one heartbeat away; may he rest easy.

Not long after Grampa Reed's death, Charles popped the question, and I accepted. I was 23 and fast becoming

an old maid. He was 24. Charles and I married in December of 1965. My 22nd move was to a one-bedroom love nest in Southeast Washington, D.C., where we

Charles and Me began our marriage. Mama kept Tonya to give us privacy. We had the weekend, and we took one day off from work. It was paradise. The following month, a friend gave us a wedding reception. It only lasted about an hour because it began to snow and stick on the ground; we wanted our guests to get home safely.

The snow became the blizzard of 1966 and dumped more than 12 inches of snow on Washington, D.C.

> *Something else was comin'*
> *The blizzard was an ill omen.*
> *There was trouble in paradise;*
> *It was something about rice.*

A few days after the reception, a woman called our apartment to tell Charles his baby boy needed his daddy. Many wished us fruitfulness, but it was not supposed to be with another woman. How could he have married me, knowing a woman was pregnant with his child, or perhaps she had the child before we married? I never knew when the baby was born. Charles said she had told him she had a miscarriage. We had known each other for over a year and a half, and he never mentioned having a girlfriend. Charles turned to alcohol.

Our marriage ended in about 90 days, but not because of the baby. I called him on his job, and he was not there. I was concerned and called our apartment, thinking he might be ill. He answered the phone and said, "If you want your things, you better come to get them. The landlord will evict us tomorrow. I am moving out now." He had intercepted an eviction notice and did not tell me. I hung up, reserved a U-Haul truck, found two helpers, and requested leave. When I got to the apartment, my husband was gone. My 23rd move was back to the home of my parents. They had moved from 10th Street, NW, to Jay Street, NE. I was devastated! I called Mary; she was supportive as always.

Charles visited often for about a year, and we talked. He said he made a mistake, but he loved me, and we could work it out; he would make it up to me. He felt we owed it to ourselves to honor our vows and not to give up on our marriage. He said he was being a father to his son, and he wanted me to understand. He asked me to reunite with him. I asked Mama to keep Tonya while we tried to revive our marriage; I wasn't comfortable taking her with me. Mary cheered me on.

My 24th move was to an apartment where Charles resided, not far from where we had lived. It took a short time to realize Charles was drinking excessively. Then I caught him stealing from my purse to support his drinking habit. I could have dealt with the baby, but his drinking and stealing were too monumental to handle. The reconciliation ended, and there was no chance of another.

> *The charmer had turned to alcohol;*
> *He was about to take a fall.*
> *At age twenty-five,*
> *He was in a nosedive.*

Daddy had purchased a house diagonally across the street from Jay Street on 57th Place when I returned to my parent's house. That was my 25th move. It was the first house Daddy had purchased since he married Mama; he had always rented. I wondered why Daddy had not bought a house and settled down during my primary and secondary school years. I believed he moved to punish me, but did it have to be for all of my school years? At any rate, I decided against asking him about his timing. That was in the past. I needed to get a divorce and increase my earnings to find a place for me and my daughter to live. Tonya would begin first grade in the fall, and I was 24 years old. It was time to leave home.

A coworker of Mary's recommended a divorce attorney named R. Kenneth Mundy, and Mary passed the information on to me. He took my case and explained the divorce process. (He ultimately became the number one criminal attorney in Washington, D.C., best known for defending Mayor Marion Barry.) I was 24 and had already had three heartbreaking relationships with Jimmy, Paul, and Charles. Whether or not it made sense, Aunt Clo's second-toe theory was at least one explanation.

After my failed marriage, I gave up on love; I had struck out with Jimmy, Paul, and Charles. I wanted a companion, but I was no longer interested in sex. I wanted platonic relationships. When the topic of sex came up, I moved on to another. I also found contentment in gospel, R&B, and doo-wop music and entertainment venues. I praised and worshipped God when I listened to Gospel music. It was uplifting. Listening to R&B and doo-wop, I experienced the ups, downs, and in-betweens of love through the stories in the lyrics. Music and entertainment took my mind off of myself and my pain.

While waiting for my divorce decree, on April 4, 1968, my boss announced that someone had gunned down Dr. Martin Luther King Jr. in Memphis, Tennessee. An ambulance rushed him to the hospital. I prayed for God to spare his life. I was driving home from work with the top down on my convertible Chevy, and the dreaded news about Dr. Martin Luther King, Jr. was announced over the radio, ending all hope for his survival. Looting and burning started right away. By the time I drove into my parents' driveway, looters had thrown cartons of cigarettes into my car. I did not know what to think about how some people were reacting to Dr. King's death; I felt a tremendous loss.

> *From the highest mountain range,*
> *Dr. King called for change:*
> *"Let Freedom Ring"*
> *Preached Dr. King.*

TWELVE

ON MY OWN

I received my divorce in the summer of 1968. The following year, Great-Aunt Louise Jones-Martin passed away from complications of diabetes (1890–1969). As her namesake, she would live on in me. She was gone but would never be forgotten. Therefore, I did not place her in one of the chambers of my heart. 1969 was also the year that Arthur Lee, Daddy's nephew and namesake, came for a brief visit. He was en route to his hometown, Memphis, after being discharged from the Army. He was the first male I had met in my Daddy's family. The tall, attractive, articulate man spoke slowly and distinctly. I loved hearing him talk.

In 1970, a few months after Arthur Lee left, I was finally ready to move from my parent's house. I had been able to save my money since my final separation from my husband, as my parents had charged me very little to stay with them. I would never know whether I could make it until I tried. I was 28 years old and my daughter was nine.

Before leaving, Aunt Clo encouraged me to go to college at night so that I might eventually make more money. In 1966, Congress chartered Federal City College (FCC) as the first public liberal arts college in Washington, D.C. The only requirement was a high school diploma or an equivalency certificate; no entrance exam was required. [7] Because the timing was right, I followed Auntie's advice. Without FCC, I probably would have been unable to attend college; passing the college entrance exam would have been an issue. Just before leaving home, I applied to FCC.

My 26th move in the summer of 1970 was to an affordable one-bedroom apartment in a low-rent community in SE Washington, D.C. I felt that was the best I could afford. Alongside my bedroom was an alleyway where drunks gathered and rolled dice, cats meowed, and dogs barked on Friday and Saturday nights. I napped those nights to make it through the next day. Thankfully, I was young and did not need a lot of sleep. I got a part-time job at the Woodward and Lothrop (Woodies) department store in the Eastover shopping center, Mondays through Fridays, for three hours at night after work and eight hours on Saturdays. I needed additional work to purchase comforts for my apartment.

---

[7] Wallace Roberts, Change and Prospects in Education," https://www.jstor.org/stable/40160965 Accessed February 5 2023

Seven come eleven blues,
They rolled the dice to win or lose:
I was on my own,
What a milestone!

Tonya stayed with Mama until school started in the fall. Mary and her family had relocated a few blocks away. Tonya lived at Mary's during the week, and her mother sent her to school. Mama kept Tonya on the weekend. Tonya and I spent a few hours together on Sunday afternoons when I picked her up from Mama's before taking her to Mary's for the week.

I purchased necessities and some comforts for my apartment, and in less than two months, a burglar broke in and stole small kitchen appliances, stereo equipment, my television, and clothing. Luckily, I was at work, and Tonya lived with Mary during the week. I reported the incident to the police, who demonstrated how the robber used a credit card to gain entry. The landlord put another lock on the door the following day, and a credit card could no longer be used to open the door. I felt safer. Before long, I picked up my mail from Mama's, and FCC had accepted me for the next quarter starting in January. I would attend night classes.

I had just replaced most of the items stolen before, and I was burglarized again while at work. That time, the thieves used a crowbar to gain entry. They took the door off the hinges. The police officers propped the door back on the hinges to make it appear closed and patrolled my street throughout the night. Although the landlord replaced the door in the morning, I feared being burglarized again. I decided to look for another place to stay.

> *Robberies ran a tally,*
> *And drunks gambled in the alley:*
> *I had to find a better place to lodge;*
> *It was past time to get out of Dodge.*

I called Mama, and she told me about affordable two-level townhouses in Dutch Village, a community up the hill from the house they recently purchased in

Palmer Park, Maryland. She said she had not heard of any burglaries in the area. The house Daddy purchased on

Clarica 57th Street had too many steps *Jones*

for Mama to enter and exit because of her heart condition. The house in Palmer Park had no steps. I applied for a two-bedroom townhouse in Dutch Village; I was approved. Aunt Clo's twin, Clarica, and her husband, Leepoleon Jones, lived in Palmer Park.

The first week of January, I moved into my 27th residence. Mary introduced me to a furniture maker and all-around handyman she knew. He installed a deadbolt lock on my front door. Then, he placed a security bar of wood in the patio door track to prevent a break-in. I felt safer at my new location. When he finished securing my new home, he built a two-person bar in my living room for a housewarming gift. He gave me the address of a place that specialized in making chic bar chairs, which could be put on layaway. I put two beautiful bar chairs on layaway.

In addition to moving to a safe neighborhood, I needed to know my daughter would be safe while I worked during the day and attended school at night. Tonya was ten years old and too young to be home alone; therefore, I asked Mama if Tonya could live with her. Mama said yes. She and Nee-Nee attended the same school. Tonya spent some weekends with me.

Now that my daughter and I had a more secure living arrangement, I quit my part-time job at Woodies and began college at FCC in the winter quarter of 1971. I decided to pay out-of-pocket instead of applying for a student loan. I would take two classes at a time. Progress would be slow, but I would eventually finish free of student loan debt. The college admissions office tested me and required me to take remedial Algebra I and II, the courses my high school teacher at Tech chose not to teach. He felt they were unnecessary for students who weren't interested in college. I was surprised that I passed both courses with a grade of B. After I completed the remedial courses successfully, I began to earn college credits for my studies.

In my second-quarter French 101 class at FCC, I met an attractive, student named Alice. Long, curly, thick black hair surrounded her face. She wanted to be a doctor; I had not decided yet. Alice and I witnessed an unforgettable scene in that French class. A homeless man wandered into the classroom and sat on the opposite side. He was eating a can of something with a

Alice

spoon and dozed off to sleep with the spoon mid-air on the way to his mouth. We responded with muffled laughter. I had to go to the bathroom to compose myself. Alice and I never analyzed the incident; we thought it was funny.

Soon after I met Alice, Aunt Eva Cloteal "Clo" Cooper-Irvine departed Earth with Lupus on April, 1971. Doctors knew little about the disease in 1971. Aunt Clo was the first of Mama's siblings that I met. She was also the sibling I spent the most time with. She encouraged me to go to college, and she was my confidant. She was also my exercise competitor when I was a teenager. I stored her in my first heart chamber, along with her father and my grampa Reed; may she sleep in heavenly peace.

I missed my aunt,
She was my confidant:
Too soon she went away
On that April day.

During my third quarter at FCC, I was shopping one Saturday and ran into an ex-coworker named Ralph. We had worked together at USDA in 1963. He said he left the USDA shortly after I left and relocated to California. He was in Washington, D.C., for the weekend to celebrate his parent's 35th wedding anniversary with them. He had made dinner reservations in an upscale restaurant and invited me to join the occasion; I accepted. His parents were gentle people, and they enjoyed the evening.

Ralph dropped his parents off at their house after dinner, and we proceeded to my place to chit-chat. I talked about being in college and how my life had changed since I left the USDA. Ralph then bragged about having become a pimp and welcomed me into his flock. I laughed at what I thought was his attempt at making a joke. Suddenly, Ralph pounced on me, pulled my dress up, and began unzipping his fly! I asked if I could go to the bathroom first. He demanded, "Make it quick!" The bathroom and Tonya's and my bedrooms were upstairs. Without his knowledge, Tonya was home for the weekend and was asleep in her room. I climbed the steps, awakened her with one hand over her mouth, and signaled her to be quiet. I whispered to her to call the police, lock her door, and remain in her room. I hurried down the steps and unlocked the front door on my way back to the living room. I further diverted the rape by suggesting that we have a drink; he accepted.

I heard a knock on the door and yelled, "Come in!" Two policemen came to the living room. Ralph tried to run. He might have escaped through the patio door, but the block of wood the handyman had placed in the track prevented him from opening the sliding door. He was trapped. Both policemen grabbed him, and I told them my story. Ralph was silent. The policemen asked me if I wanted to press charges. I said no; I just wanted him out of my house. They told Ralph to leave Maryland and never come back. Tonya had dialed 911, went back to sleep, and slept through the ordeal.

Everyone left, and I sat at my bar and poured a glass of wine to calm my nerves. I felt violated, angry, and scared. How could running into an ex-coworker have ended that way? I also felt stupid for inviting a man I barely knew into my home. For that reason, I did not tell anyone about the attempted rape. I didn't press charges because I was sure the authorities would not have believed me. I was thankful I had averted being raped. I was glad I didn't have to explain to Tonya what had happened. The next day, I told her that I asked her to call the police because I thought I heard someone out back. She never knew I had company.

★ ★ ★

In the spring of 1972, I obtained a secretarial position at the Council of the District of Columbia (D.C. City Council), the legislative branch of the D.C. government. Although my shorthand speed was slow, my boss allowed me to enroll in Strayer Business College for one

Shirley   hour twice a week to increase my speed. My dream had come true; I was a secretary, but now I had college to pur- sue. I met two invaluable coworkers, Gwyn and Shirley (1940–2010). As I was   *Gwyn* unfamiliar with working in a political organization, they helped me to adapt. We stayed in contact over the years.

> *My high school dream came true,*
> *But I had a new goal to pursue:*
> *I had started college*
> *To gain more knowledge.*

When I started working at the D.C. Council, I had earned a year of college credits at FCC and decided to transfer to a college closer to where I lived. I wanted to get home earlier at the end of my final class. Therefore, I applied to Prince George's Community College (PG) in Largo, Maryland. I was accepted in the fall of 1972, and I got home more than an hour earlier, three nights a week. However, on the flip side, I lost a few college credits because of the difference between FCC's quarter system and PG's semester system.

During the winter school break at PG, I fractured my left ankle running across the street in high heels.

Paul

DeeDee

I hobbled back to my car and drove myself to the hospital. I ended up in a soft cast and needed crutches to walk. Uncle Buster, temporarily on leave, transported me back and forth to work until my ankle healed. It was difficult to believe that nearly 19 years

Emanual
"Manny"

Peaches

had passed since Mama and I returned from West Virginia, and I first met him in January of 1954. After that time, we had only seen each other over the years at occasional family get-togethers and a few visits. My accident provided the opportunity for us to spend time together daily, as he drove me back and forth to work for several weeks. He had two children in 1954, Barbara and Doll. He now had five additional children: Paul, Clare "DeeDee" (1961–2022),

Emanuel "Manny" (1962–2005), Paulette "Peaches," and Johnny. (Barbara and Doll were pictured earlier.) After Uncle Buster brought me home from work, a classmate

Johnny   picked me up and drove me to and from PG. It took about six weeks for my ankle to knit back together.

In December 1973, Congress passed the Home Rule Act for Washington, D.C., allowing the city to elect its mayor and council. Up to that point, the D.C. Council had been an appointed body. After Home Rule, the council reorganized into various units. I became an employee in the records and legislative services unit. I received a promotion.

Next, I graduated in May 1974 with an Associate of Arts from Prince George's Community College. Although it took three years, I graduated with honors. I thanked God that Congress had chartered the FCC in 1966 so that I could go to college. I began my bachelor's degree program at the University of Maryland University College (UMUC) in the fall. I was still unsure of a college major, but I chose business because advisers told me it was a good field.

In the summer of my final year at UMUC, Daddy decided to move to Memphis, Tennessee. He had worked ten additional years after retiring from the military and wanted to change his lifestyle. All of his siblings had passed away except for two nieces who resided in Memphis. Before Daddy left, I asked him if he was my biological father. He responded, "I was with your mama during that time." In other words, he didn't know. There was no need to pursue the question any further.

Daddy

> *Mama's Baby,*
> *Daddy's Maybe:*
> *I still didn't know*
> *What was true or faux.*

Mama did not want to live in Memphis and decided that she and Nee-Nee would stay behind, although Daddy made them welcome to go. Daddy left for Memphis the following week. In a few months, Mama threw in the towel, and she and Nee-Nee joined Daddy at the end of the summer of 1976. Tonya and I were without Mama being nearby for the first time. I was 34, and Tonya was 15.

Four months after my family moved to Memphis, I earned a BS from UMUC in December 1976. Although it took nearly six years, I did not owe a student loan. I was saddened by Aunt Clo's death and Mama's inability to attend my graduation. My next objective, though not immediately, was to earn a master's degree.

THIRTEEN

MOVED FOR NAUGHT

Bearing gifts, Tonya and I drove to Memphis, TN, to visit my parents for Christmas 1976. We arrived on

Joella, Courtesy of Joi Wyatt

Christmas Eve and planned to stay for five days. Daddy's nieces, Joella and Ruth, "Sugar-Baby," came to greet us. They were accompanied by Joella's children, Arthur

Sugar-Baby, Courtesy of Joi Wyatt

Lee and Annie May. Arthur Lee kissed me on the cheek, and *Joella* shouted, "Get away from him; stop kissing him!" I was dumbfounded. Lee told me to

Arthur Lee

ignore her, but I knew she was insinuating that Lee and I were not kin. By the way, Arthur Lee was the same nephew and namesake who had visited Daddy in DC in 1969. Annie

Annie May, Courtesy of Joi Wyatt

May and I stayed in contact over the years.

The insinuation from my other side
Further confirmed my feelings inside:
I was a stepchild
And not a biological child.

We celebrated Christmas as a family the following day. We opened gifts, cooked, talked, ate dinner, played music, and Mama did her truckin' dance. The day after Christmas, Nee-Nee rode with Tonya and me to show us some of Memphis. We saw the Lorraine Motel, where the assassin shot Dr. Martin Luther King Jr. in 1968. We passed by a riverboat sitting on the Mississippi River. Graceland, Elvis Presley's home, was a large white mansion with four columns. Wrought iron gates surrounded the estate. The front yard was festive with an array of Christmas decorations. Elvis was alive in 1976, but we did not see him. The last place we drove by was Stax Records, the recording studio of soul singers Otis Redding, Rufus and Carla Thomas, Isaac Hayes, Sam and Dave, the Bar-Kays band, and more. From the outside, it looked like a movie theater. Stax had ceased operations the previous year.

On our fourth day in Memphis, Nee-Nee took Tonya to visit her friends, and an unimaginable unraveling occurred between my parents and me. Daddy said, "Lou, your mama wanted me to tell you something." (He still called me Lou.) He told me he married a woman named Pearlina in Arkansas in 1935, and when he married Mama, he had not divorced her. My mouth opened wide. Daddy continued: "Pearlina was a mean woman. She sent me to the store one day, and I kept going and joined the Army." He explained that married people in his era seldom divorced. A partner needed grounds and proof to get a divorce. Daddy said, "Had I got caught with your mama, it would have been bad." I found a web article by historian Carl Allen that corroborated Daddy's story.[8]

> I recall a couple living down the road from us who were always arguing. He was a big man, and she must have weighed about one hundred pounds. Well, one night after he came home from running after some hussy as she called her, he went to bed. While asleep, his wife sewed him up in a sheet and beat him with the buckle end of a belt. Then she just up and left. Later, they found her and carried her to court, but the court didn't do anything to her. In fact, that poor feller paid the cost of court proceedings and carried his spunky

[8] Carl Allen, "Divorce Carried a Definite Taint in Olden Days," Lakeland Ledger, August 14, 1986, https://news.google.com/newspapers?nid=1346&dat=19860 814&id=kqpOAAAAIBAJ&sjud=lfsDAAAAIBAJ&pg=6619,5720422&hl=en (accessed June 18, 2016).

little wife back home with him . . . (para. 10-11). Back then, a person had to have good grounds to get a divorce. A person couldn't just say that her husband or his wife was doing something. They had to prove it to the judge . . . (para. 12).

Pearlina and Daddy's nieces had been friends long before Daddy married Mama. She kept them updated every time she tracked Daddy and found him. She was unaware they were passing the information on to their uncle. Why did she think Daddy moved every time she learned where he was? Daddy shook his shoulders and chuckled. He didn't know either. There was more to the story. Daddy found out that the officiant who married them had not filed the marriage certificate with the court, which was the law when he and Pearlina married. Hence, their marriage was not legal. He was not a Bigamist. I was speechless. All of the moves and the many schools had been for naught.

> Daddy's nieces were like Nancy Drew.
> Whenever they got a clue,
> They knew what to do.
> They quickly informed their nephew.

After learning the reason we moved so often, several of my questions were cleared up. For example, I asked

Daddy if he knew about the technicality in 1967, when he purchased the house on 57th Street in Washington, D.C. He said he had just found out a few months earlier. I was right to question why Daddy had bought a house in 1967 rather than when I was still in school so that I could have a stable life. It was also clear why we moved from T Street to Harvard Street in 1959 instead of waiting to move directly to Fort Belvoir. His wife had tracked him down, forcing him to move before quarters were ready at Fort Belvoir. I also asked why he had not told me sooner. Mama said she didn't want me to know; it was shameful.

I also learned why Mama did not try to stop Daddy from moving so much. Mama knew about Daddy's marital status from the beginning. She said she needed health benefits because of her heart condition, and marriage to Daddy gave her that and other benefits. She said she could not say much, but she had convinced him to wait until the middle or end of a school year before we moved except once. Daddy did not know why it had taken Pearlina three and a half years to find him when we lived on T Street.

When Daddy married Mama, he said he had no grounds to divorce his wife. He said, "Your mama needed medical attention. I loved your mama and felt sorry for her; I wanted to take care of her. The military would not provide health benefits unless I married her."

It might have been a beautiful, tangled love story if I had not been a part of their love triangle.

> *The cause was bigamy,*
> *Not to punish me.*
> *I had been wrong*
> *For so long.*

Although the reason had changed as to why we moved, the cruel beating, Daddy's cold-heartedness toward me during my school years, and the seeds that family members on both sides sowed still left me feeling that he was not my biological father. Something inside of me yearned to know who my birth father was. My parents' disclosures cleared up much about our life on the move; however, the issue of my paternity remained. I asked my parents again about my paternity. They provided nothing new, and my gut feelings had not changed.

The disclosure was not finished. Mama provided another twist. She told me she heard from someone in Evington that her ex had obtained a divorce. It turned out that Mama married Daddy in October 1948, and her divorce was not final until December 1948. For years, Mama thought Daddy was a bigamist. In the end, she was the bigamist, as it turned out that Daddy was not legally married when he married Mama. It was like a Hollywood movie titled Bigamy, Double Bigamy, and a Technicality.

How did I feel about my parents' disclosure regarding the many moves? My parents did not express any regret regarding my losses and how their moving from place to place affected me. Their concern was not getting caught. They saw their responsibility as feeding and clothing me, protecting me, and seeing that I finished high school. My need for stability, connection, social, and other needs were never considered. For instance, I did not have the chance to learn how to play the piano, improve my singing, or pursue other interests. I ended up a lonely person inside because of the many losses I experienced from the moving. However, the damage was done. There was nothing I could do about what had happened to me. I had survived.

> *I had not tried to detect*
> *Any cause and effect.*
> *I had kept my mind*
> *busy, as if to spellbind.*

Although unrelated to moving and bigamy, Mama also told me she had recently contacted vital statistics in West Virginia and learned that her youngest brother, Charles Marshall Cooper, had passed away on November 3, 1972. No one provided another point of contact to the mental hospital after Grampa Reed passed away in 1965. Therefore, the hospital was unable to notify the family of his death. Uncle Charles had lived 20 years following the botched lobotomy in 1952.

I was glad my parents waited until Tonya and Nee-Nee left to talk to me about our residential mobility. Daddy had stopped moving from place to place when they were four and five. Furthermore, Tonya had no reason to believe he was not her biological grandfather. As I had no proof to the contrary, only my gut feeling, I saw no need to share my thoughts with her. Nee-Nee was Daddy's biological daughter, and she did not know that I suspected that I was not. Therefore, there was no need for them to be involved. Tonya and I spent one additional day in Memphis and headed home. Neither Arthur Lee, Joella, nor Sugar-Baby paid another visit. Annie May and I stayed in contact until her passing in 2016.

FOURTEEN

COHABITATING WITH JIMMY

On the drive home from Memphis, my mind was on Tonya; Joella's behavior had sparked a fire in me. Tonya would be 16 in a few weeks, and Jimmy had not acknowledged his daughter. I had told Tonya who her father was, but he needed to corroborate it. I wanted her to meet her father. I didn't want her ever subjected to the kind of behavior Joella had subjected me to.

On my second day home from Tennessee, I got busy trying to locate Jimmy. In July 1960, Jimmy sent me to Washington, D.C., from St. Louis, Missouri; that was the last time I had spoken to him. Otherwise, I had only seen him briefly when Mama took him to court just before Tonya turned two years old. Since I didn't know whether he was still in the military, I wrote to the Pentagon to seek a forwarding address. The Pentagon sent me his mother's address in Puerto Rico. I wrote Jimmy a five-page handwritten letter and included my telephone number. I recalled that Jimmy was a Catholic. I asked him if he thought God was pleased with him regarding Tonya.

> *Joella lit a fire*
> *To my dormant desire.*
> *Unlike the secret held by my mother,*
> *I wanted Tonya to know her father.*

Two months after leaving Memphis, violence erupted where I worked. Gunmen seized the building on March 9, 1977. At approximately 2:30 pm that afternoon, I exited the elevator on the second floor after taking a late lunch. As I walked to my office, a co-worker yelled, "Everyone get in your office and lock the door." Councilmember Marion Barry and Maurice Williams, a WHUR reporter, must have boarded the elevator after it returned to the first floor. They went to the fifth floor, and when the elevator door opened on the 5th floor, a gunman shot and killed Williams and shot Barry in the chest. He staggered into the D.C. Council chamber, where he collapsed. He survived. A guard was also shot that day, and he later died. Police officers escorted hostages on the second floor out of the building before long. I was grateful to be alive. I was 34 years old and could have been killed if I had needed to go to the fifth floor for some reason after returning from lunch. The WHUR reporter was only 24. The ordeal was surreal.

Within a month of the seizure of my workplace, Uncle John Reed "Buster" Cooper, Jr., died of lung cancer on April 2nd (1919–1977). I placed him in my first heart chamber along with his father and sister. I was thankful for the time Uncle Buster and I spent together when he transported me back and forth to work when I fractured my ankle. I also remembered Uncle Buster teaching me to stir a car. We had not spent a lot of time together over the years. Uncle Buster, Aunt Clo, and their mother passed in April.

> *Uncle Buster was kind to me,*
> *Although we related infrequently.*
> *I remembered him fondly;*
> *May God bless him grandly.*

After Uncle Buster's passing, three months had passed and I had not heard from Jimmy. I gave up hope. Then, two months later, in June, Jimmy called and showed up at my front door along with his brother. He handed me the letter I had written and introduced the man as Pedro. I introduced Tonya to her father and her uncle. Tonya displayed no emotion. Jimmy's and his brother's stay was brief. Before leaving, Jimmy asked me if I would bring Tonya to meet his wife. I reluctantly agreed, and he gave me their address. He and his wife lived in Virginia.

Tonya and I drove to Jimmy's house the following

weekend to meet his wife, Virginia. It was an awkward moment. We engaged in meaningless chit-chat, and as Tonya and I prepared to leave, Virginia invited us to a cookout in her yard the coming weekend. I again reluctantly accepted. Jimmy was quiet throughout the visit. He joined his wife in walking Tonya and me to the door.

To my astonishment, Virginia had invited his family from Puerto Rico: his mother, another brother, and his son from his first wife. Jimmy's mother could not speak English, and neither Tonya nor I spoke Spanish. Jimmy did not offer to interpret. I figured out that the purpose of the cookout was not to get to know Tonya but rather to shine the spotlight on Jimmy's infidelity. When I received his letter in Germany saying he was married, when I was waiting to deliver our baby, I questioned then how six months had been enough time to get a divorce and be remarried. Tonya said nothing about any of it; she seemed indifferent. We left after I figured out what was happening.

Jimmy called the next day, and I asked him why he didn't introduce Tonya to her grandmother, uncle, and half-brother. He explained that his mother opened the letter I sent him in Puerto Rico, got someone to translate it, and then forwarded it to Virginia. He admitted that Tonya was his daughter, and Virginia and his family were mad. I had been blindsided about the purpose of the cookout. Jimmy apologized, saying he was in the middle and didn't know what to do.

Before we hung up, I told Jimmy I was in the process of moving because management had stopped keeping the community well-maintained. I told him I had rented a U-Haul truck that I could only drive forward; I couldn't back it up. I asked him to help me. He said he would drive the rental. He then told me he and his wife were separating. I had often closed my eyes over the years and visualized him motioning me to the dance floor at the NCO club, in 1960. I also thought about my mother's involvement. I had yearned to be with him for many years. But, he had lied and disregarded Tonya and me. I had mixed emotions. Even so, I wanted him to get to know his daughter. I invited him to move in with me.

Jimmy and Me

My 28th move was to a two-bedroom apartment in Cheverly, Maryland. It was about the same price as where I moved from. Jimmy and his brother helped me move. It felt wonderful to be with Jimmy at last. Jimmy told me he had already divorced his Puerto Rican wife and was married to Virginia the night we met. Jimmy explained that Virginia was a nurse who worked six nights per week. Her one night off was Saturday. He lied to me about working late on Saturdays; that was when he and Virginia went to the NCO club. We went on Sundays. When he sent for me to come to DC from St. Louis it was to ask me to live with him until he got his divorce and then he would marry me. There was no need to tell his wife about Tonya and me after my mother's talk with him.

Finally, I knew the truth. It reminded me of Sir Walter Scott's words from his 1808 poem Marmion: "Oh, what a tangled web we weave when first we practice to deceive." It was one feeling to hear the truth but another when no apology followed. Hearing the truth without compassion for what I went through was not enough. Reality set in. Besides his wife didn't forgive him. Why should I?

> Reuniting was a mistake,
> I hit the brake:
> Sixteen years was too long;
> Too much had gone wrong.

After hearing the truth, I decided it was too late for us. We could not fix what had happened in 1960. Our baby was 16 years old; too much time had passed. We decided to become a family for three months so Tonya could get to know him. We would then go our separate ways. I was grateful that Jimmy had finally acknowledged his daughter and was getting to know her. As my Huckleberrya friend always said, "Everything happened the way it was supposed to."

At the end of three months, Jimmy and I parted ways. As he was leaving, I asked about his friend, the USO bandleader that I sang with at the NCO club. Jimmy said he didn't know; he lost contact with him. I saw Jimmy a few times over the years. He and Tonya kept in contact. I stayed out of their relationship. I did not try to orchestrate it. I brought them together, and I bowed out. She was old enough to do what she felt. Tonya never expressed any feelings about her father, and I never asked. I had done all I could do.

> *We decided to part;*
> *It was too late for a new start:*
> *Our path had been insane,*
> *There had been too much pain.*

After Jimmy and I went our separate ways, I sought to achieve my goal of earning a master's degree. I learned about a Master of Arts degree program that Central Michigan University (CMU) was offering. It was a one-year accredited off-campus night program in Washington, D.C. I was accepted. Studying helped me forget the whole Jimmy ordeal. The truth was hurtful, even though years had passed. I earned an MA in business in May 1978. There was no graduation program; the university mailed my degree. My daughter enlisted Mary's help and threw me a surprise graduation party. I was surprised! There could have been no better graduation celebration. My next goal was to pursue a PhD.

Not long after I received my master's degree the D.C. Council replaced electric typewriters and word processors with personal computers. I could easily format my document, correct errors, print, and more. Word processors had some of the same features but computers were more advanced. The personal computer greatly improved my life in the workplace. Before computers existed in the workplace, I had to type council resolutions and laws on legal-size paper without a typographical error; my boss did not accept corrections. The computer corrected typographical errors, and there was no way to know that it ever occurred. It was like magic.

> *The computer was unbelievable;*
> *What it could do was inconceivable:*
> *It made a typing correction*
> *Without detection.*

FIFTEEN

HOME OWNERSHIP

My supervisor left in 1979, and I was promoted to the position. I was able to purchase a home. My 29th move was to a semi-detached house in SE Washington, D.C. The pantry kitchen allowed for a good-size formal dining room and living room. A staircase led to three bedrooms and a bath on the second floor.

My first home

The two-bedroom basement sold me on the house, with its glass brick bar in one room, although I had to order another bar chair as the bar was a three-person

Glass Bar and Chairs

bar. The room was spacious. I purchased a futon sofa-bed so that if I needed to rent the basement out for income to make ends meet, I could turn the basement into a studio apartment. In the second room was a kitchen, bathroom, and exit door. Out back was a shed, off-street parking, a small concord grape arbor, and space for a small food garden.

Over the next 26 years, there were many notable happenings as I lived in what I thought was my permanent residence. Ten of them were, volunteering my service, the birth of my granddaughter, my 25th Tech high school reunion, seeing Paul from Germany again, planning an Evington family reunion, my Huckleberrya friend's death, the loss of my job; my second and third marriages; and meeting Diz and Millie Russell of the legendary Orioles vocal group. Their well-known song was "Crying in the Chapel."

I had a desire to do volunteer work in 1980. I learned that the District of Columbia Citizens Complaint Center needed volunteer mediators to resolve disputes involving families, neighbors, businesses, and employee/employer disputes. I applied, was accepted, and trained. The same year I began volunteer work, Aunt Ollie Florence Cooper-Jones had a heart attack and passed away on her birthday (1933-1980). She was only nine years older than me. Unfortunately, we had only seen each other two brief times after she and her family moved to Denver, Colorado, in 1955. In loving memory, I placed Aunt Florence in my first heart chamber with her father, sister, and brother.

Me holding my granddaughter

Mama holding her great-granddaughter

Four years into volunteer public service, Tonya married and left home, and my first and only granddaughter was born on July 15, 1984. Tonya named her Rachelle in my honor. I was overjoyed. Everyone called her Rachelle except Daddy. He nicknamed her Birdeye because he said she didn't miss seeing anything.

My parents had recently relocated from Memphis, Tennessee, to Alexandria, Virginia when Rachelle was born. Because of health issues, they needed to be closer to family. They were delighted to be present when their great-granddaughter was born.

Jimmy and his granddaughter

Rachelle beginning to walk

Daddy shook his shoulders and chuckled like he did when he saw Tonya and Nee-Nee for the first time.

I was a grandmother,
A position like no other:
She was like a beautiful swan,
and she would carry my name on.

The year after Rachelle's birth, Uncle James Willie "Bill" Cooper passed away (1924–1985). I have never forgotten Chubby, my first furry friend he gave Mama in 1953 when we came from West Virginia. Uncle Bill and I had a memorable start when we first met. But, over the years, we lost that connection. Uncle Bill became a wino. One of his favorite sayings was: "Give me to-da two dollars so that I can get me some to-da pluck." May he rest in peace. I placed Uncle Bill in my first heart chamber, along with his father, brother, and two sisters.

September 1985 was my 25th McKinley Tech high school reunion. I asked Daddy if he would be my escort, and he accepted. Daddy wore his fancy, dressy pants from his era, with a contrasting suit coat and tie. I took my Tech yearbook with me. I was surprised to see Sudie from T Street as she graduated a year before me. Daddy and I joined her at her table and learned that she had mar-

Daddy and Me at Tech's 25th Reunion

ried a man who had been in my homeroom at Tech. I had seen Sudie since we returned from Germany in 1962. Daddy remembered her, and they talked. Daddy enjoyed himself; he beamed during the Tech reunion. He chuckled and shook his shoulders all night. The celebration was a lasting memory with my dad. Sudie and I exchanged telephone numbers and stayed in contact occasionally.

The following year, on January 28, 1986, the Space Shuttle Challenger exploded in the air within two minutes after takeoff, killing the seven crew members. The space shuttle disintegrated before my eyes. In a flash, seven people were dead, and I didn't know what I had witnessed until I heard a newsman explain on television. Realizing what I had seen was horrifying.

That same year, I rode with Mary and her neighbor to Detroit, Michigan, for the 4ᵗʰ of July. The neighbor was attending her weekend family reunion. Paul from Germany was from Detroit, so I looked up his telephone number in the telephone book. He answered and came to where I was. Since we were in Germany together, 24 years had passed. His appearance had changed very little; he looked great. We exchanged small talk in his car, and then I asked why we had not married. He dodged the question. I had nothing further to talk about after that. I told him I had to get back to my friends.

> *I asked why we didn't marry,*
> *When he returned from Germany.*
> *My inquiry met with rejection.*
> *Paul chose to avoid the question.*

Seeing Paul in Detroit was disappointing. I should have left him in my past. The hope of learning a justification from him for having hurt me in 1962 did not materialize. At least I was no longer deluded that there was a reasonable explanation for Paul having hurt me. In Germany, When Paul played the Miracles' vinyl record, "Shop Around" he told me he had stopped shopping around when he met me. I concluded that I was only his girl away from home. I had no desire to see Paul again.

For some reason, after seeing Paul, I wanted to know more about myself and my extended family. I planned an Evington homecoming. Our last one was in 1957. Locating family members and planning took more

Mama

Mary, Tonya, and Nee-Nee

than a year. I also created a telephone book with phone numbers, addresses, and other information. Mama, Tonya, and Nee-Nee helped with the large mailings to inform the family about the when, where, and cost of the reunion. My Huckleberrya friend helped with ideas and provided moral support.

Larkin, Courtesy of Pam Watts

Mary

My Evington cousins, Larkin and Mary, who lived in Evington, the son and daughter of Cousin Eunice, who kept me as a child, were instrumental in its success. Larkin negotiated a block of rooms at the grand Raddison Hotel in Lynchburg, the closest large city to Evington, a Friday night meet and greet,

Rachelle in the lobby of the Raddison Hotel

and a banquet. Cousin Mary was the principal of the Yellow Branch Elementary School in Rustburg, adjacent to Evington, and provided space for us to have a family meeting on Saturday morning. Then, she organized a picnic at her house on Saturday afternoon and provided the food and drinks.

Following the picnic on Saturday night, more than 100 family members attended the banquet. They came

Helen

Tony Martin, Courtesy of Kenneth Martin

from as far away as California, New York, and Michigan. Clarica, Aunt Clo's twin, and Helen, the daughter of Mama's first cousin, Forest Jones, hosted the banquet with me. Tony, the son of Watsie and Beatrice "Bunchy" Martin, videoed each family unit. Watsie was present the day I was born. We honored family members, awarded gifts, broke bread

Watsie

Bunchy, Courtesy of Kenneth Martin

together, connected with new family members, reconnected with old members, and created family memories. After everyone ate, the younger family members danced until the banquet was over. Our family reunion ended the next day after church service at Chapel Grove Baptist. We ate, fellowshipped, hugged, and said our farewells. Mary mailed me a commemorative plaque the following week.

> *There was not another reunion, unfortunately.*
> *However, Tony videoed our family history.*
> *Most family members who attended have died,*
> *But what a joyful gathering it was on this side.*

Following the reunion, I continued my quest to learn who I was. I requested my primary and secondary school attendance records. Although 27 years had passed since I graduated from high school, I received information from almost all the schools. They were superb information and memory aids for addresses, my age, dates I lived there, and more when I decided to write my memoir.

* * *

My huckleberrya friend's doctor diagnosed her with cancer the year after the reunion. After chemotherapy, she was cancer-free. In celebration of her remission, in 1989, we spent a week in a chalet in Canada in an area called La Chaumine in the Laurentian Mountains near Montreal. We shopped in Montreal, Canada, and rode in a horse-drawn carriage to see a few of the breath-taking Catholic churches Montreal was known for. Afterward, the carriage driver recommended a restaurant for dinner, and our waiter told us about a nightclub for dancing. We danced the night away with Canadian students under strobe lights. We went sightseeing for the rest of the week, which included a drive to Québec City, about 300 miles away. It was a peaceful, open country drive. On our last day, we drove to Toronto and Niagara Falls on the

Me and Mary in Montreal

Canadian side. On the way home, we took several exits and shopped until there was no more room in the car to put anything. It was an unforgettable vacation together.

At the end of the summer, I went on a three-day Caribbean trip to Montego Bay, Jamaica, with another friend; Mary had to work. The trip was billed as Sun Splash time in Montego Bay and included a night of reggae music. There was also a tour to Ocho Rios. We stayed at the beautiful white-sand beachfront Holiday Inn. I also went snorkeling, and there were straw cabanas on the beach for eating, drinking, and shade.

One year and a half later, I lost my job because the chairman of the D.C. City Council ran for mayor and was defeated. His last day in office was December 31, 1990. My job ended with his. The agency called it an excepted service issue (further explanation would take another book). However, I was eligible for retirement with a substantial penalty. I was three years shy of the 30 years required to receive full retirement benefits; I was three years shy. I refused to retire; I walked away on faith. I was determined to find another government job to earn a full retirement.

The loss of my job was frightening, being a single person. However, I had fantastic memories of my years at the Council. For instance, the annual Christmas parties, celebrities that stopped by, and the Redskins Super

Bowl XXII football celebration. The Christmas parties consisted of socializing and food and drinks galore. A few famous people who stopped by were Queen Elizabeth II and her entourage, who walked down the hallway of the D.C. City Council in 1976; Motown's Temptations and Supremes; Jerry Butler; the Soul Children; and football professional and entertainer Rosie

Art Monk and me Grier. I got the opportunity to talk to them. The Washington Redskins bested the Denver Broncos 42 -10 in 1988. I met Doug Williams, the first Negro quarterback to start, finish, and win a Super Bowl, and coach Joe Gibbs. Handsome wide receiver Art Monk, the quiet man, took a photo with me. The Redskins became the Washington Commanders in 2022.

> *The Broncos were the favored team,*
> *But the Redskins reigned supreme:*
> *DC celebrated the games they played*
> *with confetti and a parade.*

After my job ended, I applied for unemployment compensation and began looking for employment. I also started collecting 45 vinyl records as a hobby. One day, while looking for vinyl records in a Goodwill Industries store, I met my second husband. We engaged in small talk, and then he followed me to a place where we ate lunch and continued to talk. I learned he was a veteran, a government employee, and we were both Southerners. Our conversation also revealed that Waldo was 13 years younger than me. We were both okay with the age difference. After lunch, we exchanged telephone numbers. The attractive young man with an outgoing personality and skin as smooth as a baby's bottom began to take me out on the town; I felt youthful. We had much in common. For example, we were both workaholics, liked occasionally browsing through relics at Goodwill, and we loved Motown music. He made me laugh when he entertained me by lip-syncing a song by the Temptations vocal group and doing their choreographed steps. We had a whirlwind romance, and after about nine months, Waldo proposed. I had long gotten bored with platonic relationships and decided to take another chance with romance. I had been single for 23 years.

Waldo and I married in November 1991 at the Upper Marlboro, Maryland courthouse. My family was present. On the photo, from left to right, were Rachelle, Tonya, Mama, Nee-Nee, and Daddy. Nee-Nee planned

a small reception for family, neighbors, and a few friends at the clubhouse where my parents lived. Not all family members were on board with the age difference. *Getting Married* Three remarks were: He's only six years older than her daughter. My daughter made a toast to her mother and stepfather. Another remark was about him being a young grandfather. Waldo and I ignored the comments. We were married, and

Family Present at My Wedding

we were comfortable with our age difference.

Miraculously, I obtained a government job three months after my marriage. The U.S. Department of Justice (DOJ) held a job fair. The DOJ was looking for clerical workers to help complete a project they were working on. I sought an interview, explained my situation, and DOJ hired me in February 1992. I had no delusions of getting back into government as a manager or supervisor. Because I was eligible for retirement, I considered it a miracle to have found any government job.

One month after I started working, my Huckleberrya friend's cancer returned, and she chose not to go through another round of chemotherapy. She had been in remission for four years. Mary Jane Powell went to be with the Heavenly Angels on March 19, 1992. She didn't tell me until I saw her in the hospital during her final days. She always had an encouraging word for me no matter what situation I got into. We knew one another for 35 years and stayed in contact wherever I moved. Mary was my sister in every way but blood. I stored her away in my second heart chamber; her memory would be eternal.

> *When my Huckleberrya friend died,*
> *Heaven was more beautified:*
> *Our sisterhood was a joyride;*
> *I missed Mary being by my side.*

About a year after the death of my Huckleberrya friend, the Department of Defense (DOD) hired my husband for a job in California. He didn't tell me he was applying for a job outside of Washington, D.C., and expected me to leave my house and my miracle job and follow him. I couldn't do that. At any rate, the job was a promotion for him, and I encouraged him to accept it, although we had only been married for 18 months and my best friend had passed away four months ago. Nevertheless, he was younger than I, and I didn't want to hold him back. When Waldo left for California, I stayed behind to secure my retirement without my Huckleberrya friend, or my husband. I felt like my world had shut down.

When Waldo had been gone for about a month, I went to Roadhouse Oldies, a store on Georgia Avenue, NW, that sold classic vinyl records and other music to look for 45-rpm records. There, I met a man named Joe, who was collecting eight-track music tapes. We talked and bragged about our record collections. Then, to one-up me, Joe said one of the Orioles lived in his neighborhood and asked if I wanted to meet him. He told me that the Orioles vocal group started singing in 1948 in Baltimore, Maryland. My teen music era was the 1950s and 1960s, so I remembered their final big 1953 hit, "Crying in the Chapel." As the Orioles were legends, I was interested in meeting his neighbor and learning more about their music.

Before long, Joe called to tell me the Orioles were performing in downtown Bethesda as part of the Summer in the Parks entertainment and asked if I wanted to join him. I met Joe there, and during the group's performance, he pointed out his neighbor, Albert "Diz" Russell, as the one with the signature white patch of hair in front of his head. I was glad I attended the concert with Joe. The Orioles sounded great!

When the concert ended, Joe and I went backstage to meet Diz Russell. Instead, we met the Orioles' manager and Diz's wife, Mildred "Millie" Russell, who told us that Diz was unavailable; he was changing his clothing. Since we couldn't see Diz, she invited us to their home for a Fourth of July cookout in their backyard. I accepted, but Joe had made other plans. At the cookout,

*Diz and Millie,
Courtesy of
Mildred Russell*

several local entertainers performed in the backyard, including the Orioles. Millie's long legs, dreadlocks, and unique raspy voice were distinctive. She introduced me to Diz Russell, and they both welcomed me. Friends Neighbors, and fans attended the cookout.

> *Amid the cookout hustle and bustle*
> *I met the legendary Diz Russell.*
> *He was outgoing, jovial,*
> *And his deep voice was tuneful.*

I stayed in contact with the Russells; we became friends. Before long, they invited me to accompany

them when they performed. As such, I met many pioneers of R&B and doo-wop music. Diz became like a big brother. He was knowledgeable, an active listener, and had a gift of gab.

Me With Diz and Millie at a Ben E. King affair in Leesburg, VA

What I liked most about him was his non-judgmental personality. I grew to admire and respect him, and I wanted to do something for him. He told me he had done almost everything, so I asked if he had written his life story. He answered no. I volunteered to do it, and he agreed. I told him it would take some time; I had not written a book before. He said he was in no hurry.

About that same time, I met a woman named Noreen while going around with the Orioles. Her storytelling manner of talking, along with her body language made her an excellent communicator; she always had stories to tell. She and I became friends and remained friends over the years.

SIXTEEN

MOVED
SECOND HUSBAND

While hanging out with the Russells and waiting for retirement, I learned of a seminar in Arlington, Virginia, regarding a PhD program that had recently begun at The Graduate School of America (TGSA) in Minneapolis, Minnesota. I attended. The program was not accredited. However, it sounded like an excellent program. I believed it would be accredited. I liked the program. Obtaining a PhD was my goal when I earned my master's degree in 1978. The timing, on the other hand, was not in my favor. I was waiting on a retirement buy-out that was rumored to happen any day. I would then join my husband in California.

While hanging out with the Russells and waiting for retirement, I learned of a seminar in Arlington, Virginia, regarding a PhD program that had recently begun at The Graduate School of America (TGSA) in Minneapolis, Minnesota. I attended. The program was not accredited. However, it sounded like an excellent program. I believed it would be accredited. I liked the program. Obtaining a PhD was my goal when I earned my master's degree in 1978. The timing, on the other hand, was not in my favor. I was waiting on a retirement buy-out that was rumored to happen any day. I would then join my husband in California.

Next, on August 7 Aunt Clo's twin, Theresa May "Tee" Irvine passed away (1948–1994). She was six years younger than I. An aneurysm in her brain burst. She had recently undergone a physical exam and got a clean bill of health. In retrospect, she had often complained of excruciating headaches, "Lou, my head hurts me so bad." She and her sister, Clarica, were the only twins in the Cooper family. Mama and I had spent lots of time at Aunt Clo's when they were young. Too soon, God called Theresa home. No more pain, rest in God's arms.

In December 1994, the DOJ offered the buyout retirement package I had been waiting for. After working on my miracle clerical job for almost three years, my government employment journey finally ended. With 30 years of government service, I retired in 1995, at age 52 with full government retirement benefits and a bonus. Faith in God, determination, and perseverance paid off. I was finally free to join my husband in California.

I got back into the government.
I earned a full retirement.
Thou somewhat backward
In the end, I moved forward.

Before joining my husband in California, I began working on the story of the Orioles vocal group. I promised Diz three years earlier that I would write the book. I interviewed Diz and everyone else who had sung as an Oriole, except one I could not reach. Then, I conducted a literature search at the Library of Congress. In addition to Diz and Millie, I stayed in contact with the other Orioles that I interviewed. They have all passed away now, except for Ray Apollo Allen, Larry Jordan, and Richard Dunbar. Ray and Larry have continued to perform, and I have continued to attend their performances.

I had gotten the book started, and it was time to join my husband in California. Noreen helped me to plan a goodbye party. Amongst others, Diz, Millie, Gwyn, Sudie, and Grace came. My guests and I ate and chatted, and everyone wished me a pleasant journey. Near the end of the party, Diz tried to form my guests into a choir to back him up while he sang me a farewell song. It didn't happen, but it was hilarious.

In April, I joined my husband in San Leandro, California. I had moved again, although I owned a home. It was my 30th move. As Waldo and I had been apart for almost two years and had only seen each other once during that period, I did not rent my home; I kept it available. I gave my next-door neighbor, Mr. Davenport (1914–2008), a key and asked him if he would oversee my property. He was glad to do it. I only took a few personal items and clothing.

Mr. Davenport

Our one-bedroom apartment in San Leandro had a balcony with a beautiful view; the area was close to a marina and a golf course. I was in California for about a month, and as I suspected, Waldo had another woman. I returned home. We talked by phone for the next three months. He said he was lonely without me and it would not happen again. He said he had told the woman that he and his wife were reuniting and that it was over between them. With that, I forgave him and agreed to return to California.

In September, I returned to California. In November, Waldo surprised me with an announcement that he had gotten a job in Kaiserslautern, Germany. Again, he did not discuss his decision to apply for a job abroad with me. He said he was hopeful but had not expected to get the job. He applied because going abroad would be an opportunity to get our marriage back on track. He asked me to travel with him to work on our marriage. As I was retired, I welcomed returning to Germany. We had been apart for nearly two years, and our marriage was off track; I agreed to go.

> *It was an opportunity,*
> *To work on unity:*
> *There was no denying,*
> *It was worth trying.*

Waldo hitched our belongings to his Cherokee jeep in a U-Haul truck and drove us cross-country from California to Washington, D.C. Our first stop was in Las Vegas, Nevada. We played the slot machines for a while and then proceeded to El Paso, Texas, where I shopped before we walked across the border to Ciudad Juarez. Then we drove to Georgia and visited Waldo's parents and brother for two days before motoring to Washington, D.C.

Our cross-country drive from California to Washington, D.C., was exciting, enjoyable, and memorable. On January 3rd, we obtained passports at the State Department. After deciding that one automobile would be sufficient in Germany, I decided not to renew my expiring lease. After arranging for packers to pack up our household goods, Waldo left for his job in Germany. I lingered behind to decide what furnishings to take to Germany and what to leave in storage. I also had to rent my house out. I did not rent the basement; again, I hedged my bets. I did not feel comfortable about my marriage. If it didn't work, I wanted to have a place to live until the lease expired. The renters would deposit a rental check in my bank account each month. My daughter agreed to take care of other business affairs and housing repairs.

Waldo picked me up at Frankfurt Airport in June 1996. We drove by the 97th General Hospital, where Tonya was born. A wrecking crew had demolished it in the early 1990s. I felt sad that a piece of my history was gone. We continued driving to Kaiserslautern, Germany, known as K town, where Waldo was employed. K Town was about an hour and a half from Stuttgart by car, where I had lived in 1960.

Waldo was not eligible for military housing. Although he worked for DOD, he was not in the armed forces. He was living in a hotel. We found an advertisement in the Stars and Stripes military newspaper for an

Our Apartment Bldg.

apartment that became my 31st address. We moved in the same day that I arrived. The comfortable two-bedroom apartment with a kitchen, living room, and balcony became our home. The large picture window in the kitchen was the focal point for me. After we received our household goods and were settled, I sat at the window and wrote Mama, Tonya, Nee-Nee, and a few friends to give them my address. Nee-Nee had married a soldier, and they were on a tour of duty in Hawaii.

Although Waldo was not eligible for military housing, the military allowed us to shop at the Vogelweh military commissary and the Ramstein Base Exchange. We could also attend the NCO club and play bingo, slot machines, and other activities. As I had grown up a military dependent, those facilities were familiar; I had missed them. Those were the places Waldo and I went on weekends. One additional venue was a bowling alley with slot machines. Almost everywhere had slot machines; they were plentiful in Germany.

> *The military culture was unique,*
> *Returning to it was a special treat:*
> *Growing up as a military brat,*
> *I enjoyed returning to that.*

Within two months, I knew without a doubt that coming to Germany, as far as my marriage was concerned, was a mistake. Waldo came in from work most days and started an argument. I agreed to come to get our marriage back on track and could do little about my plight, so I decided to pursue the PhD program I inquired about before retirement. I refused to waste three years arguing with Waldo. I needed to add meaning and purpose to my life,

Me in K Town, 1996

something I could do alone. I applied for the program. The college admissions officer interviewed me in December, and TGSA accepted me into the program. Unbeknownst to me, the seminar I attended in Virginia was a prerequisite to application.

A few days after TGSA accepted me in their PhD program, Tonya informed me that Jimmy had passed

away in Puerto Rico (1933–1996). He had returned home when he retired from the military. Not having married and raised our daughter together made me

Tonya and her dad, Courtesy of Tonya Adams

Tonya

sad. However, I was grateful he had eventually acknowledged Tonya, and they got to know one another. I had come to the understanding that we had met in 1960 to give me my amazing daughter. All was forgiven; I wished him eternal peace.

The following July, TGSA provided seminars at a university in St. Paul, Minnesota that I needed to take advantage of because I was having difficulty getting started in the program. I flew there. My daughter joined me. I was thrilled that the university allowed her to join me in the dormitory. We had not seen each other in seven months. We dined at night, went sightseeing, and shopped at the Mall of America. We also found two Native American-owned casinos nearby to go "ching-chinging," as Nee-Nee called it. We passed by the entrance to the entertainer Prince's house, but his house was hidden from the roadway.

Upon my return to Germany, I had a better idea of what I needed to do. I needed access to a library and a German driver's license. The library was not close to where I lived. K town didn't require a road test because I had a valid United States driver's license. I studied and learned the road signs and traffic rules, took a written examination, and obtained a driver's license. On the days I needed to use our car, I dropped Waldo off at work and picked him up. I was finally able to begin my studies.

I studied and prayed in front of the large picture window in our kitchen. Returning to school after 20 years was challenging, but my studies kept me busy and gave me purpose. The view of old, tall, alluring green trees was stunning and soothing. I saw children playing and families walking together around the neighborhood. I felt safe alone in the apartment during the day; it was a quiet neighborhood. I prayed to endure an unhappy, quarrelsome marriage.

On August 31, Princess Diana died in an automobile crash at age 36, the same age as my daughter. She was the epitome of the Cinderella story: a commoner who married a prince, the myth, the fantasy, the symbol of love and happiness. Because of her marital status at the time of her death, although her issues were more complicated, I felt a kindred spirit with her. I cried for her and myself.

> *Our marriage was yakety-yak;*
> *It did not get back on track:*
> *It reached the point of no return,*
> *And I made a U-Turn.*

Following Princess Diana's death, despite my prayers, the bickering between Waldo and me reached the boiling point. After being in Germany for 15 months, the marriage was over; it was time to go home. I called the military and the German police. I also called a female soldier I met at the NCO club, explained what was happening, and asked her if I could spend the night at her house. She said yes and came to get me. One of the officers helped me put a few items in her car.

I spent the night with the soldier, and the next day, I called Beth and Brad, a military couple that Waldo and I also met at the NCO club and who lived in the same military housing area. I knew them better than the soldier who picked me up. Beth was a soldier, and Brad was her husband. Brad answered the phone, and I asked if he could pick me up. The Army's military housing area was large, and I didn't know how to walk to Beth and Brad's house. They were entertaining friends, but he picked me up anyway. He and his wife introduced me to their visitors, Abby, and Allen. I explained my situation, and Beth and Brad invited me to spend the night with them and their visitors. Allen drove his large pickup truck to visit Beth and Brad, and the next day, he took me to my apartment, where I retrieved the remainder of my small items. I had to leave my furniture because I could not ship it home. The military would ship it when Waldo returned to America. Thankfully, Waldo was at work.

When we returned to Beth and Brad's, I noticed men delivering boxes of household goods to a military family in the housing area. I followed them to the recipient and asked for a few of their cardboard boxes once they had been emptied. They said I could have them. While I waited for them to unpack, Beth and Brad allowed me to put my belongings in their storage bin in the basement of their apartment until I could pack them. The next day, the neighbor gave me several of their cardboard boxes. I packed everything, and Brad loaded the boxes in his truck and hauled them to the post office for shipping.

Having shipped my goods, I obtained accommodations at the military hotel in Ramstein. I called my renters to notify them that I was returning home. I asked if they would put my cardboard boxes in the basement when they arrived. I also wrote my parents, Nee-Nee in Hawaii, and my close friends to let them know I was returning to America. It had been a long four days; I was tired. I ate and went to sleep.

I had a few more tasks to complete before I could leave Germany. After breakfast the next day, Brad drove me to complete tasks such as returning library books and going to Klaber Kaserne's legal services to inquire if there was anything I needed to do of a legal nature. He also drove me to Waldo's job to tell his boss what had happened. His boss informed Waldo he had to return him to America after I told him my story. However, Waldo requested to use the six months of leave he had accrued first, and his boss approved the request. In retrospect, had he requested leave and had taken me on the honeymoon we never had, our marriage might have had a chance. Despite what could have been, it didn't happen. I finished everything I needed to do and made reservations to fly to Washington, D.C., on September 29, 1997. Tonya would pick me up at the airport.

Once I was ready to leave Germany, I called Beth and Brad and asked Brad if he would drive me to the airport the following morning. Allen and Abby were getting ready to return to their home in Belgium. I thanked them and Beth and Brad for their help. Everyone was glad they could help me. Without the four of them and my initial soldier friend, who picked me up when I left Waldo, I don't know how I would have been able to leave Germany. Thank God for them!

Brad drove me to the airport on September 29, 1997. I could finally exhale. Eventually, I lost contact with Beth and Brad and the soldier who picked me up the night I left Waldo. Abby and Allen also lost contact with Beth and Brad. Abby and I have corresponded at Christmas time every year by e-mail. Allen passed away in 2022.

As Waldo and I failed to unify,
To Germany, I said goodbye.
Being with him had become insane.
Auf Wiedersehen!

SEVENTEEN

ABROAD SECOND TIME
RETURNED TO THE USA

When I arrived home, 21 months remained on the 36-month lease of my house. Thank God I had hedged my bets and had not rented the basement. I was serene and peaceful in my cozy studio apartment, even if I had shared it with many cardboard boxes containing my belongings. I was grateful that I was home safe and healthy and that I had used my time wisely by returning to college to obtain a doctoral degree. The ordeal in Germany showed me how strong I was. That was my 32nd move, even though it was back to my house.

> *By not renting my basement,*
> *I minimized my displacement:*
> *Thankfully, I hedged my bets,*
> *And avoided further regrets.*

I had two immediate items to check off on my agenda. First, I needed to purchase a car to get around in. Second, I needed to find an attorney to begin my divorce procedure. I called Noreen, and she drove me to a Chevrolet dealership, where I purchased an Impala Chevrolet. At the car dealership, I ran into an ex-coworker who gave me the name of an attorney; she raved about his legal expertise. He took my divorce case but explained that he could not file papers in Superior Court for six months because six months of residency were required in Washington, D.C. Because I lived abroad for more than a year, I had to re-establish residency. It was perfect that Waldo remained in Germany for six months. I could serve him with divorce papers as soon as he returned to America.

Feeling that obtaining my divorce was in capable hands, I phoned my few friends and learned that my T Street pal, Almeta, passed away while I was in Germany. The last time I saw Almeta was at Mary's funeral. I was saddened. I had known her since 1957, and I hadn't gotten the chance to say goodbye.

Next on my agenda was to take my parents to their medical appointments to relieve Tonya, who did everything for them while Nee-Nee and I were abroad. I also began to visit Daddy one or two nights a week. He was eighty-nine, and Mama seldom missed playing bingo at night. Daddy welcomed the company. I usually stayed until Mama came home, and we played cards.

We played for ten cents a game and chased dimes for hours. We enjoyed playing cards as a family.

Along with visiting my parents, I returned to my studies. The Higher Learning Commission granted The Graduate School of America accreditation. The institution then changed its name to Capella University. I made the right decision to trust that the program would be accredited. I would receive my degree from an accredited university. The news motivated me to increase the time I worked on my degree to complete it faster. It was a blessing that I lived in Washington, D.C., where I could conduct research at the Library of Congress, the largest library in the world.

* * *

Waldo returned to Illinois in April 1998 and called to tell me I could pick up my furnishings. He also released the items I had put in military storage. I rented a Ryder Truck and boarded an Amtrak to Illinois. Tonya and a friend, Wayne, rode with me on Amtrak to help me load and drive my household goods home. I also asked Wayne to serve Waldo with the divorce petition. He was a Washington, D.C. resident, and the Superior Court of the District of Columbia required service of process to be performed by a D.C. resident. Wayne agreed to do it.

Waldo picked us up at the Amtrak station, took us

to pick up the Ryder truck I had rented, and then led us to a garage where my furnishings were. There, Wayne served him with the divorce papers. Waldo grabbed my arm and said he wanted to speak to me. I pulled away and told him to talk to the judge. After loading everything, Wayne, Tonya, and I alternated driving to Washington, D.C. It took forever to get home because a car governor regulated the speed. Tonya and Wayne kept portions of my furnishings at their homes for over a year. Tonya also housed the furniture that Waldo released from government storage.

> *Thankfully, my daughter and Wayne*
> *Came along to Illinois on the train:*
> *They helped to retrieve my furnishings*
> *And to serve Waldo for our divorce hearing.*

While waiting for my day in divorce court, an ambulance rushed Daddy to the hospital after a fall, and a surgeon performed emergency head surgery. After the surgery, he did well for about two weeks before his condition worsened. Arthur Clay eased away without regaining consciousness with his family at his bedside (1907–1998). He was interred at Arlington National Cemetery with a 21-gun salute. I wished Daddy eternal peace and stored him in my third heart chamber.

The following month, a judge granted my divorce. Waldo drove from Illinois to be present at the hearing.

One pleasant takeaway was the cross-country drive from California to Washington, D.C., when we were preparing to go to Germany. Unfortunately, we went to Germany to bond but grew further apart.

> *The Judge granted the decree;*
> *And joyfully, I was free:*
> *I moved on to complete my degree;*
> *It took my mind off of Germany.*

The year after my divorce, Aunt Margie's children brought her to visit Mama from Philadelphia. When

Reginald

Mama, Terry, and I stayed with Uncle Jesse and Aunt Margie in Philadelphia in 1956, they were the parents of four children: Gwen, Horace, Terry, and Ronnie (pictured earlier). They were ultimately the parents of nine. The other five were Doretha, Reginald, William Thomas, Vanessa, and Patricia. Aunt Margie had developed Alzheimer's, and her

William Thomas, Courtesy of Terry DeVaughn

children wanted her to spend time with her only sibling while she still knew her. She and Mama were the last two of ten children. Aunt

Doretha, Courtesy of Sharon DeVaughn

Margie and I only saw each other a few times in life. She and her family moved to Philadelphia in 1955, the year after I met her for the first time. When Aunt Margie visited Mama, she knew her and me, although her Alzheimer's disease was in an advanced stage. Aunt Marjorie "Margie" Marie Cooper-Devaughn re-  turned to Philadelphia at the beginning of the millennium and passed away later that

Patricia

Vanessa

year (1929–2000). I placed Aunt Margie in the first chamber of my heart along with her father, two sisters, and two brothers; may she rest eternally.

Near the end of the millennium, Nee-Nee's doctor diagnosed her with cancer. She and her husband had returned from Hawaii to Texas. Her doctor hospitalized her at the Medical Center in San Antonio, Texas, and she and her husband lived in a nearby Fisher Foundation house that built homes for military and veteran families to stay free of charge when a loved one was hospitalized. [9] In July 2001, the Fisher Foundation allowed me to spend two weeks with my sister and use all the facilities free of charge. I was appreciative. It was an essential service for my sister and her husband during their time of need.

During my visit, my sister and I confessed our love for each other and discussed her relationship with God.

---

[9] About Fisher House Foundation, "Fisher House, Helping Miltary Families," nd, https://fisherhouse.org/about/ (accessed January 30, 2023).

She told me she had joined a Baptist church nearby and had been baptized. Nee-Nee found the strength to take me to her church. She wanted me to see that she was worshipping and praising the Lord. She was well-known and loved by everyone in the church, especially the pastor and first lady. Nee-Nee had turned her life over to God.

As I packed to leave San Antonio, Nee-Nee told me Mama was unaware of the severity of her illness and asked me not to tell. She moaned, "I can't deal with Mama's sadness and tears. I am trying to fight this disease." I promised not to tell. If she wanted Mama to know, it was her call. I regretted that our nearly 20-year age difference made it difficult for me to relate to her as a sister. She and Tonya were like sisters; they were 14 months apart. I was grateful to have spent two weeks with my sister.

Shortly after I returned home from Texas, the abysmal call came. Getting Mama to Texas was problematic. Her doctor had put her on oxygen after being diagnosed with Chronic Obstructive Pulmonary Disease (COPD). The airlines did not allow oxygen tanks, and Amtrak would have taken hours to get

Rachelle

to Texas. Tonya decided to drive to San Antonio. The family rode together—Mama, Tonya, Rachelle, and me. When we arrived, Nee-Nee was unconscious. Mama spent the night in her hospital room. The next day, Wanda Cloteal Clay-Griffin surrendered to cancer on August 5, 2001. Because her husband was an active-duty soldier, the military interred Nee-Nee at Arlington National Cemetery in Arlington, Virginia. She and her father rested there. I placed my sister in the fourth chamber of my heart; may she rest in paradise.

Mama blamed me for not telling her that her baby was dying. I had spared Nee-Nee more agony; it was her call to tell Mama. "A gossip betrays a confidence, but a trustworthy man keeps a secret" (Proverbs 11:13, NIV). There had been much pain between Mama and me for many years. After my sister's burial, I went on a hiatus.

I honored Nee-Nee's wish,
To spare her more anguish:
My emotions were raw;
Mama's blame was the last straw.

The following month, on September 11, 2001, I was on leave from work and eating breakfast, when I turned on the television to watch the news. An airplane had crashed into one of the Twin Towers of the World Trade Center buildings in New York City. I assumed the pilot lost control of the plane. In about 15 minutes, another plane hit the second tower. Oh my God! The United States was under attack! A third aircraft smashed into the Pentagon in Arlington, Virginia, and hero passengers downed a fourth airplane in Pennsylvania, perhaps headed for the White House or U.S. Capitol. I prayed for the families and friends of the people who died on 9/11, and I thanked God for the first responders, miracle survivors, and heroes. That day and the weeks that followed were horrible! I returned to my studies to ease my mind.

Two years later, I completed my dissertation, and in April 2003, Capella awarded me a PhD in education. I

did not attend the graduation ceremony in person; I watched it on simulcast. Mama did not see me graduate because I was estranged from my family. I was disheart-

Dr. Clay   ened. I wanted us to be together when I proved to those women who had talked behind her back and called me a burden when I was a child. On the positive side, my studies carried me over plenty of troubled waters. The university mailed my degree, cap, gown, and collar.

In celebration of earning my doctorate, my FCC classmate, Alice, whom I met in 1971 in French 101, treated me to dinner at a restaurant of my choice. She also gave me a bold cherry wood frame for my degree and a high five. It was mind-boggling that 32 years had passed since I began my studies at FCC. Alice became the medical doctor she aspired to be and earned a PhD. It took me much longer, but I eventually made it to the finish line. My future goals were to get an upgrade done in my house that I had put off and to complete the Orioles book I had delayed.

> *Although as slow as a turtle*
> *I jumped over the hurdles.*
> *It was a slow climb,*
> *But I made it in time.*

EIGHTEEN

MOVED
THIRD HUSBAND

The upgrade I wanted in my house was a counter between my kitchen and formal dining room, so I could eat small meals and snacks without eating on the large dining room table. It entailed taking down a portion of a wall that housed electrical wires. My neighbor referred me to her contractor, who had done something similar in her house. His name was Miles. We talked as he and an electrician worked on the project over the next few weeks. He was a widower with three grown children, a Christian, and a retired government worker who had started his own home improvement business some time ago. He was eight years older than me.

The easygoing, petite man completed the job in my home and invited me to attend church with him. I accepted. He picked me up the following Sunday, and his polished Stacy Adams shoes and stylish suit and tie caught my eye. In addition to attending church on Sundays, we soon began attending Bible study on Wednesday nights and going out to dinner and other places.

> *Miles was older;*
> *Waldo had been younger:*
> *Was the older man*
> *The better plan?*

By September 2003, Miles and I had known each other for about four months, and he invited me to attend a family fish fry in South Carolina. He said he was driving there Saturday morning and returning the same day. He asked me to accompany him, and I accepted. His family welcomed me and made me miss mine; I had not seen my mother and daughter since my sister's burial in 2001.

On the way home, as we neared the exit where my daughter lived, I asked Miles if we could stop by her house. He said yes, and I called her. Mama answered the phone; Tonya wasn't home. I told Mama we were on our way there. Mama opened the door, and we hugged. I introduced her to Miles. Mama told me she was living with Tonya. I did not react, but I was shocked that Mama nor Tonya had conferred with me before moving Mama out of her apartment. Even if we were estranged, I was Mama's next of kin. Miles and I stayed for a half-hour, and Tonya did not return. We left. It had been an enjoyable fish fry; however, the one-day trip was tiring. We were anxious to get home after the long drive.

I called Tonya the following day and made plans to bring Mama to my house for a visit. Miles and I picked her up from Tonya's the following week-end, and he met my daughter. I was glad he had met my mother and daughter. I assumed Mama was ill, and Tonya moved her to her house to care for her. I chose not to bring it up. It was done, and I wanted to keep the peace and move forward. Neither of them mentioned it either. We needed to mend.

Tonya

> *I wanted to avoid another calamity;*
> *Because I had missed my family.*
> Time to travel a new lane
> More sunshine, less rain.

On Mama's first visit, I wanted to show her how I planned to care for her. I bathed her and put lotion on her body, prepared food, and we ate together. Her appetite was poor, and her body was frail. She had become dependent on Ensure food supplements. She consumed a little more when I ate with her. While eating, I talked about the good old days when I was growing up; we had some laughs.

On Mama's second visit to my house, we attended an affair her church was sponsoring at Fort Myer Army

Post on October 24, 2003. Mama had returned to church about ten years ago. The affair was titled *A Christian's Night at the Apollo Talent Showcase Banquet and Dance* and included a lavish buffet. It contained gospel singing and praise dancing. In retrospect, it was as if God had taken Mama and me back to the beginning of our life together when we attended gospel concerts. It was a wonderful evening.

On the second day of Mama's visit, she stared into space and declared, "I wonder where we'll be next year this time." In the past, Mama had jokingly told me she would be here to cut the lights out. I reminded her of that vow. With a half-laugh, she uttered, "I might be cutting them out a little sooner." I dismissed it: "Ahh, Mama, you're not going nowhere." We embraced, confessed our love, and admitted we had hurt one another. Mama then congratulated me on my PhD. As circumstances had prevented me and my family from being together at my graduation ceremony, the validation warmed my heart. I asked Mama again who my biological father was. She stuck to her story that he was Arthur Clay. She added, "If he's not, I will take it to the grave.

Mama visited again in November, and we were comfortable spending time together. Following that visit, Tonya and I agreed I would pick Mama up on Sunday, December 7, to bring her to live with me. I felt it was my responsibility to take care of my mother. At 1 a.m.

on Saturday, December 6, the telephone awakened me. Tonya was trying to adjust Mama's oxygen so she could breathe. I listened helplessly as her COPD took its toll. Paramedics arrived and administered CPR to revive her. Tonya and I agreed that Mama did not want medical personnel to take further measures to resuscitate her. Mary Everene "Rene" Cooper-Clay transitioned at age 78 (1925–2003); may she rest forever in the light.

It was ironic that Mama had a heart condition most of her life, but advanced COPD was the cause of her death. Her words on November 22 about cutting the lights out replayed in my brain. Had Mama foreseen her death? I regretted that Mama did not get to live with me; however, God did not mean for it to be. Additionally, I regretted that Mama took the identity of my biological father to her grave. I had a right to know!

On the other hand, I was grateful for her love and protection as I grew up and for being a second mother to my daughter. Above all, God gave me the time to tell Mama I loved her. Mama was the sole survivor of her nine sisters and brothers. Therefore, as she jokingly said for years, she had lived to turn the lights off amongst her sisters and brothers; none of them lived to be an octogenarian.

Mama joined her husband at Arlington National Cemetery, reuniting him with his beloved May-ree, as he called her. Nee-Nee was buried nearby. Grampa

Reed, Aunt Clo, Uncle Buster, Uncle Bill, Aunt Florence, and Aunt Margie were stored in my first heart chamber, my Huckleberrya friend in the second, Daddy and Mama in the third, and Nee-Nee in the fourth. They all rested one heartbeat away in my four heart chambers. May all of their souls rest in peace.

Two months after Mama's death, Miles proposed; I said yes. However, we waited another year, until June 2005, before we married; he did not want to rush. Miles'  Cousin and her husband gave us a wedding reception at their house. Tonya, other family, friends, and church members attended the reception. Additionally, I had run into Joyce from T Street and my Crystals vocal group a few weeks before my marriage, and she was present. I had lost contact with Joyce for many years.

Joyce

> We dated for a year, were engaged for one,
> Met family and had loads of fun:
> We wanted our marriage to grow,
> So, we took it slow.

I moved in with my third husband, my 33rd address. His house was a detached single-family brick house with four bedrooms and a basement. I liked it, except the three bedrooms on the ground floor were small, about 12x12. As Miles was a contractor, I asked if he could enlarge them. He informed me he could not enlarge the rooms to the extent I desired without rebuilding the house, and there was not enough land available. For that reason, we also sold his house and left the city.

We found a lot in an active adult community in Fredericksburg, Virginia, to have a home built by Ryan Builders. I was thrilled to be purchasing the large house of my dreams. The day we selected our house from the available models, we chose it from an architectural drawing on the wall. Miles could read the blueprints, and he liked that one; I yielded to him since I couldn't read the drawing. There was no model for the architectural drawing, but he assured me it was sizeable. Further, we drove around the community and saw many beautiful, large houses. Therefore, I surmised the blueprint could not have been much smaller.

Ryan Builders completed our home in May of 2006. Miles had driven to Fredericksburg twice to look at the construction of the house; I stayed home and waited to see the finished product. My 34th abode had one sizeable master bedroom with a walk-in closet and an adjoining bath. The other two rooms were 12x12 and 10x10. We sold his house because the rooms were about that size, and I had complained that they were too small. I was disappointed.

Our Newly Built House

At any rate, the purchase was a done deal. Miles had put down the most, although I had added a sizeable amount.

Miles said we would soon be mortgage-free. I, on the other hand, wanted a large house. I was not interested in not having a mortgage payment. I was willing to pay half the mortgage. I was dumbfounded at how I could have allowed it to happen. However, as we had been married less than a year, I told myself it was only a house.

Our house was off US Route 1, not far from where Great-Aunt Dorothy died in the car accident that occurred in 1962 while I was in Germany. I went to the library to learn more about what happened and found an article in the Fredericksburg Free Lance-Star. [10] The article dated Thursday, March 8, 1962, reported that it had snowed nine inches on Monday and another six inches on Tuesday. A truck rammed into their skidding car near Massaponax, Virginia. Great-Aunt Dorothy and her husband, Uncle James "Shep" Sheppard, were returning home from a funeral in North Carolina. Uncle Shep survived. I was glad to learn what had happened to her.

> *Auntie breathed her last breath*
> *As they returned home from a death.*
> *What a tragic irony*
> *For Great-Aunt Dorothy.*

---

[10] Paul Muse, "Injured Baltimore Man Taken from Auto After His Wife Was Killed," Free Lance-Star, March 8, 1962.

Shortly after we moved into our new home, a colleague from Capella University recommended me for an online adjunct teaching position in the business department at the University of Maryland University College (UMUC). I had no desire to teach or return to the workforce; I had been retired for 11 years. However, I saw an opportunity to pay forward some of what I received from professors, and it would be an honor to teach at my undergraduate alma mater. As my master's degree was in business and my PhD in education, I applied for the job, and UMUC hired me to teach Introduction to Business Management. Online teaching turned out to be rewarding, although it had its pros and cons.

About the same time we moved to Fredericksburg in 2006, Facebook, founded by Mark Zuckerberg and other Harvard University colleagues, opened to the masses. [11] I did not get involved with the website for a few years, and then it was only in hopes that Spike from T Street might befriend me on the website. I would love to have known how his life turned out. I was also interested in reconnecting with Bessie May, Loretta, or Jessie from my past. Otherwise, because of moving, I knew few people from my past.

On the fourth of July, Miles and I drove to Bowling

---

[11] Mythili Devarakonda, "'The Social Network': When was Facebook created? How long did it take to create Facebook?" USA Today, July 25, 2022. https://www.usatoday.com/story/tech/2022/07/25/when-was-facebook-created/10040883002/, accessed July 9, 2022.

Green, Virginia, about 30 minutes from Fredericksburg, to join the on-lookers for their annual parade. After the parade, Miles and I located Union Elementary, the elementary school I had attended when we lived in Bowling Green. The city had transformed the school into the Caroline County Community Service Center. A commemorative marker read in part, "Union High School, 1903–1969." I had not stayed in contact with any classmates from Union. It was validating to see Union Elementary again, even if it was now a service center, and there was only a marker. It was sad, however, that another part of my history was gone, like the hospital in Germany where Tonya was born.

> *Time had marched on*
> *Union Elementary was gone:*
> *How the years had passed by,*
> *And I didn't have one classmate tie.*

As we drove home, Miles asked about the book I had told him I started writing in 1995. He wanted to know if I intended to finish it. The next day, I removed the

Book signing in Baltimore

manuscript from the file cabinet and began to work on it again, determined to finish it that time. It was about my friend Diz Russell and the Orioles vocal group book that had arguably started rhythm and blues music in Baltimore in 1948. I joined the Fredericksburg Riverside Writers Group and received help with my writing. I finally completed Diz's book, *The Orioles: Second String Albert Diz Russell.* (A copy can be purchased at Drrachelclay@comcast.net).

Later the same year, on November 4, 2008, the American People elected Barack Obama, the first African-American U.S. President. I canvassed door-to-door for the campaign and worked at the polls on election day. I verified and signed off on the final vote tally with the precinct captain, making my signature a part of the history of President Obama's election results in that precinct.

★ ★ ★

One Saturday in May 2009, I was on my way to the library when I spotted a yard sale. Whenever I saw yard sales on Saturdays, I usually stopped and browsed around. The sellers had Lhasa Apso dogs for sale. I viewed the puppies, and a dark brown runt of the litter stole my heart. I called to ask Miles if I could purchase a dog. He had no problem with it. The puppy had been born on May 10, 2009, and was seven weeks old when we picked him up. Miles wanted to name him Tito, and I added David as his middle name because I wanted him to have a biblical name. Tito's feathery tail waved back and forth like an umbrella. Over

Tito In Training

time, the brown dog was sometimes black. At other times, his coat, feet, and ears were a mixture of gold and silver. Tito was the first and only dog I owned. Mama owned my other furry playmates, Chubby, Diamond, and Butch, and cared for them; I just played with them.

Once, while walking Tito, I met a neighbor named Vanessa Lewis, who was also walking her dog. We often ran into each other while walking our dogs and stopped to talk. I told her I didn't like the church my husband and I were attending, and she invited me to

Pastor and Mrs Woodard, Courtesy of Mr. & Mrs. Woodard

Michelle Simms-Lewis

worship at her church, Sylvannah Baptist. The white steeple atop the church reminded me of my childhood church, Chapel Grove, in Evington, Virginia. I joined Sylvannah Baptist in 2009, where the pastor and first lady were Reverend and Mrs. Dennis Woodard. I loved the old gospel songs the choir sang and some contemporary ones; I joined the choir in 2011. Michelle Sims was the choir director. Miles attended Sylvannah with me occasionally but remained at his place of worship.

Not long after I joined the Sylvannah choir, Cousin Eunice Sylvia Thompson-Watts passed away (1912–2011) in Evington, Virginia. I attended her graveside funeral. She had kept me from age four to about age five while Mama regrouped following her separation from her first husband. Her daughter, Mary, was born in Evington and continued to dwell there.

In February 2012, Miles and I parted ways because of irreconcilable differences. My 35th address was to a luxury one-bedroom senior citizen apartment. Miles helped me to relocate and afterward he kept Tito if I needed a dog sitter. He continued to be there for me if I needed his help. Our parting was civil.

> *My first union was terminated in eviction,*
> *The second, in unaddressed tension,*
> *The third marriage was a tale of woe;*
> *Where I should go from here, I didn't know.*

NINETEEN

MOVED
FOURTH HUSBAND

My first outing after my separation from Miles was a drive to Washington, D.C., in April to see the $29 million renovated grand opening of the Howard Theater, where I went to see performances in my youth. It closed its doors permanently in the 1980s. After more than 30 years, builders revived a slice of my history. I was excited that it was reopening. I saw the inside renovation and the Howard was a dinner theater with a bar where the balcony used to be. It was too small for a dinner theater. I had expected a renovated theater where I would see entertainers from my youth, or tribute groups and individuals perform the music I grew up with. The one renovation that met my expectations was the large, nostalgic iconographic photographs of past performers that the decorators placed throughout the structure. Otherwise, the Howard Theater I had known, was gone. I attended one show and where I was sitting on the side, I couldn't see the stage well and the space in the balcony was mostly a bar. Remembering the Howard as it was; I was disappointed.

> *Although beautifully renovated,*
> *It wasn't what I had anticipated:*
> *Waiting for more than 30 years,*
> *It didn't receive my cheers.*

At the grand opening of the Howard Theater, the owner of the American Classic Woman of the Year senior pageant, Letha Blount, was recruiting contestants. For several years, she had held it in July at the historic Lincoln Theater, less than a mile from the Howard. The woman asked if I had a talent, and I told her I sang. She gave me her contact information and asked me to let her know if I wanted to compete. I called the following week and agreed to be a contender. She signed me up and gave me the address for meetings and rehearsals. I attended and competed in the senior pageant in July 2012. It was similar to a Miss America pageant, except no swimsuit competition. Five judges chose a pageant winner, crowned her queen, and awarded her a $500 prize. They also chose a first-runner-up and third-place winner. I sang Sam Cook's song "A Change is Gonna Come." Friends from Fredericksburg came along with me: Clifton and Rita, Eula, Gillie, and Gwyn and Noreen, who lived in Washington, D.C., to cheer me

on. The judges chose me as the first runner-up; I won
$250.

The same month, I cruised on the Oasis of the Seas,
a Royal Caribbean cruise ship. It was a cruise to Halifax,

Nova Scotia, and was a delayed
honeymoon for Miles and me. I
invited my longtime friend
Noreen to take his place. One
activity provided on board was
a Hula Hoop contest. I com-

*Me Hula
Hooping*

*Crowned
the Queen*

peted against younger competitors. I spun up to five
hoops around my waist. I had to keep at least one spin-
ning for a given time. I won, and the entertainment
director presented me with a bouquet and crowned me
queen. The entertainment director then tasked the
Hula Hoop audience and participants with honoring
their queen on the ship for two days by holding up one
hand, making the victory sign, and chanting "Whoop!"
"Whoop!" I loved the attention. The cruise was a lot
of fun.

Soon, another year had whizzed away, and my
two-year contract ended where I lived. I relocated to
another place because the rent increased. For about
the same amount I was paying, my 36th residence of-
fered two bedrooms, two baths, and a screened-in
porch. Additionally, it was across the street from Mary
Washington Hospital, Fredericksburg's oldest hospital.

I was comfortable in my new apartment with my trusty companion, Tito.

Soon after moving in, I came across a place that sponsored bingo on Friday nights, something I could do alone. The second week I attended, while waiting for bingo to start, a woman pointed to two seats where a couple used to sit to play bingo and announced that the man's wife had died. They were regular players. As a new player, I didn't know the individuals.

Bobby Hawkins

The following week, the man came to play bingo, and the same woman pointed him out. I thought to myself, "Hmmm, not bad." I solicited a pal's advice on how to go about meeting the handsome man. I didn't want to appear brazen. My pal gave me advice that she had read in *Our Daily Bread*, a Christian devotional. The message read in part:

> *Take the initiative.* Don't wait to be intro-
> duced. Say hello and get the other person's
> name. If you're naturally shy, it can be
> hard taking the first step. But the chances
> are the other person feels the same, and
> when you start talking, you'll find things
> in common. *Take a risk….* If everything
> works out, exchange phone numbers and
> invite the other person for coffee or lunch.

(The message was based on Ecclesiastes 4:9, NLT.)

When the man came to bingo the next time, I spoke, expressed my condolences, and revealed that I was interested in meeting him. He said he had been married for 45 years and was spending time alone to grieve. He said he had come to bingo because they had played bingo together. I told him I understood and was in no hurry. He was willing to talk by phone, and I gave the hazel-eyed, silky black-and-white-haired man my calling card. He, in turn, gave me his phone number.

Bobby and I communicated by phone for several months without contact. We had a lot in common. For instance, we were born the same year, 40 miles apart, and we liked playing cards and bingo. Contrarily, he had been married once, and I had been married three times. Bobby had one son, three grandchildren, and a brown and white Shih-Poo dog named Delilah. At the end of Bobby's six-month mourning period, we had what I deemed "breakfast at Tiffany McDonald's."

On our next date, May 2, 2015, Bobby and I attended the eighth annual Silver Prom for the 50-plus senior community. It was sponsored by the Ron Rosner Family YMCA thanks to the HeartFields at Fredericksburg senior living community. The Silver Prom was romantic with my new beau as I had not attended a junior or senior high school prom during my secondary school years; It took me back in time.

> *Our romantic evening was lovely,*
> *With plenty of food and bubbly:*
> *I attended a prom at last*
> *But with an older cast.*

A few days after the prom, Bobby told me he was uncomfortable dating a married woman. I told him that filing for divorce was a formality, as I had completed the legal matters except for the actual filing. I told him I had not filed for divorce because we had parted ways as friends, and I only knew a handful of people in Fredericksburg. I filed for divorce immediately; it was final in July.

The following month, on August 21, Bobby proposed on bended knee and proposed. I answered yes,

and we married in November in front of the Spotsylvania Courthouse. A few friends were present, as shown

Our Wedding Party

in the photo below

from left to right: Rosemary, Vanessa, her husband, Calvin, Bobby, me, and Noreen. Vanessa was the woman I met while I

Wedding Kiss

was walking Tito, who invited me to Sylvannah Baptist

church. Rosemary was also a member of Sylvannah Baptist. Noreen was my friend from D.C.

Move number 37 was to my husband's split-level, three-bedroom house with a two-car carport and a shed in Fredericksburg, Virginia. It was a corner lot with a large front and back yard surrounded by tall, beautiful trees like the ones in Germany, and other decorative shrubbery, and flowers. Bobby's Shih-Poo dog, Delilah, hopped on her hind legs and welcomed me. It was my first time knowing a Shih-Poo dog. She was smart and loving.

Delilah and Tito

She and Tito eventually got along well and became protective of each other like siblings.

The neighborhood was clean, quiet, and peaceful. Neighbors kept to themselves. We spoke to each other

Lexi and Oliver

and passed the time of day while walking our dogs for the most part. I came to know one loveable lady well. She was the neighborhood celebrity. She quickly made friends and loved playing ball with everyone who would throw the ball and play with her. The black Labrador Retriever's name was Lexi. The Cocker Spaniel was his parent's newly acquired puppy. Oliver was a small dog but fit right in and held his own.

With my fourth marriage, I had come full circle. My first marriage was coeval, the second to a younger man and the third to an older one. Bobby and I were the same age. To quote my favorite comedian, Richard Pryor, "I believed in the institution of marriage and intended to keep trying until I got it right." Pryor married seven times to five different women.

> *Joking aside,*
> *I was over being a bride:*
> *Number four was it,*
> *I was calling it quits.*

Nine months after our marriage, Vanessa Lewis, who attended our wedding, completed her earthly ministry and went to be with the Lord on August 16, 2016. She led me to the church that I eventually became a member of. I was shocked to learn of her sudden death from a blood clot in her leg. Matthew 24:36 (NIV) states, "But about that day or hour no one knows, not even the angels in heaven, nor the Son, but only the Father."

★ ★ ★

About one year and a half after my marriage, my daughter, Tonya, retired from Andrews Air Force Base in March 2017. She had a formal retirement program and asked me to sing "The National Anthem." The ushers seated the guests, and the master of ceremonies announced, "Dr. Rachel Clay will sing the National

Anthem." At the conclusion, Tonya presented me with a bouquet, and I wished her a glorious retirement and told her I was proud of her.

Two months later, my husband's doctor diagnosed him with COPD. The doctor prescribed home oxygen at night. He did not need it inside during the day or outside if he did not walk for more than two minutes. His doctor said the COPD came from smoking. Bobby had quit smoking more than 30 years earlier.

In August of the same year, my doctor found a mass in my kidney. I went to the Johns Hopkins Urology Department, and Dr. Misop Han scheduled me for laparoscopic surgery on October 17, the day before my 75th birthday. I did not reschedule; I wanted to get the mass out of me. I had faith in God that the surgery would be successful. By God's grace and mercy, I woke up briefly in recovery and fully the next day, on my 75th birthday. I was discharged the following day. The following week, Dr. Han called to tell me that the pathology report confirmed that the mass was cancer. The positive news was that he believed he had removed it all. I did not need radiation or chemotherapy.

> *Facing cancer was alarming.*
> *It was also disarming.*
> *Although it was scary,*
> *I had a successful surgery.*

Pastor and Mrs. Dennis Woodard, my pastor and first lady of Sylvannah Baptist Church, visited us. It humbled me that they cared enough to come to our home and pray for us. My husband and I were grateful. The following month was our second anniversary. We had faced serious illnesses during our second year of marriage.

★ ★ ★

After my cancer surgery, my desire to identify my biological father intensified and I joined the Ancestry.

Joi, Courtesy of Joi Wyatt

Dawn, Courtesy of Joi Wyatt

com database. When no close DNA match showed up by 2018, I attempted to rule Arthur Clay out by contacting two of his closest remaining relatives, Dawn Cox and Joi Wyatt. They submitted their DNA. They were Daddy's great-great nieces. Joi also collected her uncle Arthur Lee's DNA (Daddy's great-nephew) and submitted it to the DNA database. None of them were matches. However, DNA results can be inconclusive between cousins.[12] At any rate, because they were my sister's blood relatives, I considered them my relatives. Because of the deaths of close relatives on Daddy's and

---

[12] Cousins DNA Test, International Bioscience, https://www.ibdna.com/tests/cousins-dna-test/ (accessed November 10, 2022).

Mama's sides, chances of finding my biological father were slim, but not impossible. I was not giving up.

Two years after my surgery, I decided I had worked long enough and resigned from my job. I taught for almost 14 years; along with my years of government service, I worked for nearly 44. To celebrate my freedom from work, I purchased tickets for my husband and me to attend a Valentine's Day Smokey Robinson concert at the Metro Goldwyn Mayer (MGM) National Harbor and Casino in Oxon Hill, Maryland.

My husband was not feeling well on Valentine's Day, and I asked my friend, Corrine, to go with me to the Smokey Robinson concert. My favorite singer's voice was in mint condition, and he looked fantastic. My mind regressed momentarily to Germany in 1961, when Paul introduced me to Smokey on a vinyl record when he played "Shop Around" by

Corrine

the Miracles featuring Bill "Smokey" Robinson. It was hard to believe that had been more than 40 years ago. Corrine and I thoroughly enjoyed the performance.

A few days following the Valentine's Day concert, the unimaginable happened, COVID-19. The World Health Organization declared the virus a pandemic. Dr. Anthony Fauci, the chief medical advisor to the president, recommended that Americans wash their hands often, wear masks, and stay quarantined in their homes.

When people left their homes, they had to follow social distancing; meaning stay six feet apart. Governors and mayors imposed additional restrictions that varied from state to state.

Sadly, my T Street pal, Sudie, died from COVID-19 (1941–2020). Her friend Grace called to inform me. I remembered T Street, the Caravan, the Barnum and Bailey Carnival, the Howard Theater, and Tech. Joyce and I had lost contact. More than 60 years had passed since Mary, Sudie, Almeta, Joyce, and I met on T Street in 1957. We had some great times together. Rest in God's arms, Sudie.

Living through the COVID-19 pandemic changed American lives. Doctors closed their offices, and hospital emergency rooms were overcrowded. Many businesses also closed. My husband and I only went out of the house to go to the grocery store. We went to virtual doctor's appointments and virtual church. COVID-19 continued to cause death, destruction, and uncertainty, it became the new way of life. Thankfully, we heard of no cases of dogs dying from the disease or spreading it to humans.

> *COVID-19 was fearful and baffling*
> *Death, quarantine, masks, rationing:*
> *A vaccine was created within a year*
> *And variants became another fear.*

On November 3, 2020, amid the COVID crisis, the American people elected Joseph Biden, Jr., as the 46th President of the United States and Kamala Harris as the Vice President. Kamala, a biracial African-Asian American was the first female Vice President of America. Her husband, Doug Emhoff, was given the title: Second Gentleman of the United States. He was the first person to have that title.

Two months following the election, in December 2020, the research and development component of America's Pfizer Pharmaceutical, in the United Kingdom, created a vaccine. Moderna, an American pharmaceutical company, was close behind, followed by Johnson and Johnson. We were hopeful that the vaccines would control COVID-19. Controversial and conspiratorial theories were abundant. However, Bobby and I took the vaccines.

The following month on January 6, 2021, the Congress of the United States assembled to count the electoral votes and for Vice President Mike Pence to certify the November 2020 electoral votes that elected Joseph Biden as the new president. Donald Trump who had been elected the 42nd President of the United States in November of 2016 claimed that the Biden election was stolen. Then, a mob stormed the United States Capitol to prevent the certification. There were several deaths, many injuries, and millions of dollars in damages. As I watched the insurrection on television, I was terrified for our elected officials and our democracy.

Two years after the insurrection, life had slowly returned to a sense of normalcy and COVID-19 was not  as scary. Health officials recommended annual boosters similar to flu shots for the variants of COVID-19. On April 29, 2023, I felt safe to attend a play about Sister Rosetta Tharpe at the Ford's Theater in Washington, D.C., an early memory from

Me, Day of the Play

my past. Sister Tharpe was the gospel singer who wanted Mama to entrust me to her in 1949 to teach me to sing with her on stage. Playwright Cheryl L. West adapted the book, about Sister Tharpe's life, *Shout Sister Shout*, written by Gayle Wald, for the stage. Sister Rosetta Tharpe sang gospel and blues and, in my opinion, was one of the top voices of her time, along with Mahalia Jackson, Billie Holiday, and Brother Joe May. Who knows? Had Sister Tharpe taught me to sing on stage with her, I could have been included in that number. I enjoyed seeing Sister Tharpe's life story performed on stage.

> *I was a part of Sister Tharpe's music career*
> *At age six in 1948, a leap year:*
> *A brief chance meeting and telephone call*
> *That resulted in nothing at all.*

Not long after that play, my husband's COPD worsened. He had been diagnosed in 2017 with COPD. We had to call the ambulance every couple of months, and he was admitted to the hospital. Eventually, after three or four days at home, he had to return to the hospital. Soon, he was unable to return home.

Bobby's pastor and first lady, Reverend and Mrs. Clarence Mays, were my anchors. On Bobby's final day, Pastor Mays spent several hours in the hospital with Bobby, me, his son Brian, two nieces, and a long-term friend, Teddy Bumbrey. Although Bobby's best friend, Brother Clarence Morefield, was physically unable to be with him,

Reverend and Mrs. Mays, Courtesy of Reverend and Mrs. Mays

he called Bobby often until Bobby could no longer talk. Everyone but me had left before Bobby took his final breath. I told him I loved him, and he was free to go; I would be alright. It was difficult to witness his death alone. On August 3, 2023, my husband, Bobby Hawkins, passed away from advanced COPD (1942-2023). He was eighty. Bobby was a good provider; God would now provide for him.

Bobby's memorial service took place at A.L. Bennett and Son Funeral Home. Deacon Derrick Johnson presided, Sister JoAnne Fowler prepared the programs; Sister Joyce Webster read the obituary and the Old and

New Testament scriptures; the Union Bell choir sang, and Pastor Clarence Mays delivered the eulogy; all from Bobby's church, Union Bell Baptist. My Pastor, Dennis Woodard, and First Lady Susie Woodard of Sylvannah Baptist Church also attended. Pastor Woodard said a few words. Additionally, solos were sung by my long-time friend, Raymond Allen, and Bobby's son's friend, Shay Lassiter. This was the first time I had made funeral arrangements for someone who had passed away. Bobby's son, Brian, wrote the obituary.

Family, Church members from Union Bell Baptist and Sylvannah, and friends came to Bobby's homegoing memorial service. I was surprised to see cousin Kenneth Thompson, the grandson of Great-Aunt Amanda from Baltimore, Maryland, Grampa Reed's sister. We learned later in life that we had attended McKinley Technical High School together but did not know each other. I was overwhelmed by the outpouring of love from everyone.

On October 9, 2023, Tito David passed away. He was 14 ½ years old and was suffering from a tumor. He had given me unconditional love and was a trusty companion. Delilah went to live with Bobby's son and his family. I added Bobby and Tito to my second heart chamber along with my huckleberrya friend, Mary Jane.

In November 2023 I went to see a play titled *Up from the Ashes,* written, produced, and directed by Jack

Jacobs. Nayjah, a member of Union Bell Baptist was one of the stars in the play. It was about a family who put their faith in God and were ultimately able to move forward following the loss of close family members. The play inspired me.

In August 2024, a year had passed since Bobby went away, and 10 months since Tito died. I had mourned them, and it was time to move on. I had faith in God, and I believed that He had more in store for Little Louise. I had yet to find my purpose. My first chore was to complete my memoir. I had not worked on it for a long period of time.

> *It was time to end my grieving*
> *And move forward with living.*
> *My life was not standing still*
> *And I had God's will to fulfill.*

The last week of July 2024, President Joe Biden endorsed Vice President Kamala Harris to run for the 47th President of the United States. At first, I was ambivalent. Is America ready for a woman president? Is America ready for a black woman president? Then, Jessie Jackson's words came to mind, "Keep Hope Alive," and President Barack Obama's words, "The Audacity of Hope." Then I asked myself, "Why can't she be president?"

In September of 2024, I traveled to London,

England, for four days and spent one day in Paris, France. It was a five-day trip that seemed more like two weeks as we crammed so much in. We toured down the Seine River in Paris for an hour. Contractors had almost completed the repair of Notre Dame after the fire in 2019. We also shopped on the Champs Elysees and dined. In London, we toured in a Black Cab accompanied by a tour guide, spent an hour exploring London on the River Thames on a boat tour, went to a high tea, shopped, and dined. We also went to Windsor, England, to St. George's Chapel, where Queen Elizabeth was buried. We happened to be there on September 8, which was the second anniversary of her death. It was a wonderful trip with the Pierians, an arts appreciation group.

On November 5, 2024, the people elected Donald Trump as the 47th President of the United States of America and JD Vance Vice President. Donald Trump was the second person to win two non-consecutive terms. He was the 45th president and defeated Kamala Harris to become the 47th president. Grover Cleveland was the 22nd and 24th president. [13]

★ ★ ★

---

[13] Leslie Kennedy, "How President Grover Cleveland Won Two Non-Consecutive Terms," https://www.history.com/news/president-cleveland-two-nonconsecutive-terms

I was born in Evington, Virginia, and moved 37 times. Move <u>one</u> was nineteen months old when my mother married, and we relocated to his farm. My <u>second and third</u> moves were with two different relatives, one in Evington and the other in Baltimore, Maryland, between the ages of four and six. Then, my mother married a second time to a man named Arthur Clay, whom she said was my biological father. However, my great-aunt Dorothy, whom I was living with, did not believe he was my dad and told Mama so in my presence. I wanted a dad, so I believed Mama. At age six, Mama moved me from Baltimore to Washington, D.C., for move <u>four</u>; we became a nuclear family.

The summer after Mama married my new Daddy, he beat me cruelly and put bleeding welts on my body. The skepticism of my aunt surfaced, and I began not to believe Mama; how could he be my dad? Mama confronted him and threatened to do bodily harm if he ever hit me again. However, Mama stuck to her story that he was my biological dad.

I began school in the fall, and during Christmas school break, Daddy moved us to Fort Belvoir, where he worked. Then, when school ended in the summer, we moved again, <u>five and six</u>. Now I began to think that because Mama had forbidden my father to hit me, I began to believe the reason he was moving was to punish me because I was not his biological daughter. I cried to

Mama, but she insisted that he was my dad. We continued to move around Washington, DC, Maryland, and Virginia, once to West Virginia, moves <u>seven through 15</u>. There were many occurrences during those moves, but a few of them were seeing a telephone and television for the first time, attending gospel concerts, meeting my Grampa Reed and other family, homecomings in Evington, and meeting my best friends Bessie May and Mary Jane, my first kiss, and I was baptized. I also completed high school. By then, I had attended 14 primary and secondary schools, excluding kindergarten.

While completing high school, I learned simultaneously that I was pregnant and Daddy had asked for a tour of duty in Germany. Mama and I spent time in Saint Louis, Missouri, with my dad's sister before going to Germany. That was <u>move 16</u>. My <u>17th</u> move was to Kassel, GE., where we lived in a house with pigs in the basement. We moved twice more in Germany, <u>18th</u> <u>and 19th</u>. Mama had a second child while we were in Germany, and because of her heart condition, we returned home a year early.

We stayed with Aunt Clo in Washington, DC, until we moved to Fort Belvoir for move <u>20</u>. Daddy retired, and we returned to Washington for move <u>21</u>. Within three years, I married, separated, reconciled, and separated again for moves <u>22-25</u>. When I returned home again, Daddy had purchased a home for the first time.

I found that to be odd. Why had he not purchased a home during my school years? However, it was irrelevant. I was grown, working, and needed to get a divorce and move out on my own.

I left my parent's house in 1970 and moved three times before I purchased a place of residence for moves 26-28. During that time, I also started college. Move 29 homeownership. I earned a BS and MA degree and married a second time while occupying my home, and there were many more occurrences. Then, for moves 30-31, I moved to California and Germany with my second husband. I began to work on my PhD in Germany but left my husband before finishing and returned to my home. That was move 32.

I completed my PhD, married for a third time, sold my residence, and moved in with him for move 33. I desired a larger house, and he soon sold his home. For move 34, we moved to Virginia. Eventually, we separated, and I lived in two senior apartment complexes for moves 35-36. In three years, I married a fourth time, and for move 37, I moved in with him. I vowed my next move would be to Heaven. I had moved more than enough!

Going back to 1976, when I earned my BS degree, my parents had moved to Memphis, Tennessee. Tonya and I visited for Christmas, and that was when Daddy told me why we had moved so many times during my primary and secondary school years. He was a biga-mist, and Mama was aware of it all along. However, he learned in 1967 that because he nor the person who married them had filed his marriage certificate with the court, he was not legally married. He had not moved to punish me. We had moved for nothing.

After I learned the truth about why Daddy had moved from place to place during my primary and sec-ondary school years, I still did not believe he was my biological father. Further, relatives on both sides had inferred that Arthur Clay was not my birth dad. His distant relatives submitted DNA to a database, and our DNA did not match. However, I found information on the web that DNA results between cousins were not conclusive. With my age and the death of Arthur Clay and his close relatives, chances of locating my biological father were slim.

While moving from place to place, I had lots of fun, met a few friends, and had many other exciting ex-periences. Conversely, moving resulted in me losing playmates, classmates, two aunts and uncles, and their families. I was socially isolated, for the most part, espe-cially during my primary and secondary school years. The losses caused deep-seated loneliness within me that has remained throughout adulthood.

Writing my memoir was a catharsis. I discov-ered I had survived the loneliness by having platonic relationships, listening to gospel, rhythm and blues, and doo-wop music, and attending entertainment venues. I kept music playing in the background of my life and discovered it had been therapeutic. Further, continuing to study, having goals, and working kept my mind active and away from the pain. Also, it helped me discover that I married four times because of loneliness, which was not an outside fix. Nobody could fix the loneliness inside of me except me, with the help of God. The greatest lesson I learned from writing my memoir was that I was never alone; God was always with me. Prayer has remained the greatest weapon of all. I have vowed that my next move will be to Heaven. I hope my memoir will help others.

> *To manage my loneliness disease*
> *Prayer, music, and goals were the keys.*
> *With perseverance, I thrived.*
> *And by God's grace, I survived!*

Richard Hansom Jones, Sr., Courtesy of Carroll Jones

Richard Hansom Jones, Sr., was born on November 15, 1888, and died October 17, 1980. He was Great-Grandmother Bertha Jones' first-born son of four. His wife was Mary Elizabeth Claiborne. Their children were Marion, Massie, Richard, Jr., James "Booly," Calvin "Coots," Bayles, Mary Anna, and Viola "Lissie."

Charles Henry Jones, Courtesy of Sandra Golden

Charles Henry Jones was Great-Grandmother Bertha Jones' second-born son of four. His delayed birth record shows his date of birth as October 22, 1889, but his tombstone shows October 22, 1885, a four-year difference. He died on March 23, 1946. His wife was Mary Alice. Their children were Alexander "Elic," Virginia, Bertha, Shirley, Eunice, Thelma, Harrison, and Charles Williams (Not with Mary Alice).

APPENDIX C

Watsie Louis and daughter, Jean Jones, Courtesy of Javon Greene

Watsie Louis Jones was born on December 22, 1897, and died on December 20, 1967. He was Great-Grandmother Bertha Jones' third-born son of four. His wife was Carol. Their children were Jean and Margo. Jean is beside him in the picture above.

APPENDIX D

William McKinley Jones, Courtesy of Helen Armstrong

William McKinley Jones was Great-grandmother Bertha Jones' fourth and final son. He was born on January 28, 1902. His obituary states that he was born in 1900, but his sister Mary Ann was born in 1900. Further, his son William Thomas' birth record shows his father as age 16 when he was born in 1918. William McKinley died January 15, 1984. His wives were Gretel, Mary, and Helen. Their children were William Thomas, Herbert, William McKinley, Jr., Forest, Helen, and Ruth.

Mary Eliza Irvine-Cooper,
Courtesy of Mary Watts

Gennie Freeman-Cooper,
Courtesy of Barbara Banks

Mary Eliza Irvine-Cooper was Grampa Reed's mother and my great-grandmother. Her husband was Jack Cooper. Their children were Jack, Jr., Willie, Eddie, John Reed, Amanda, Dorothy, Jane, and Fannie.

Gennie Freeman-Cooper was Grampa Reed's grandmother on his father's side. She was my great-great-grandmother. Her husband was Weekley Cooper. They had one child, Jack Cooper.

Aunt Clo's twins and their younger sister. From left to right, Clarica, Kaye, and Theresa, who passed away in 1994 at age 45. She had one son, Steven.

Yours truly. On the left was in London, England, in September 2024, entering the London Hilton. On the right was Saturday, November 30, 2024, at an entertainment concert featuring Gerald Austin and the Manhattans at the Birchmere in Alexandria, Virginia.

Printed in the United States
by Baker & Taylor Publisher Services